D1564842

Beyond Borders

THE SELECTED ESSAYS OF Mary Austin

EDITED & WITH AN

INTRODUCTION BY

REUBEN J. ELLIS

Southern

Illinois

University

Press

Carbondale

&

Edwardsville

Beyond Borders

Library of Congress
Cataloging-in-Publication Data

Austin, Mary Hunter, 1868–1934.
    Beyond borders : the selected
    essays of Mary Austin / edited and
    with an introduction by
    Reuben J. Ellis.
        p. cm.
    Includes bibliographical references.
    I. Ellis, Reuben J., 1955–
II. Title.
    PS3501.U8A6   1996
    814'.52 — dc20   94-47456
    ISBN 0-8093-1997-7   CIP

Dedicated with love to

Dorothy Ruth Ellis,

Elizabeth Ione Ellis,

Harriet Leora Medlin,

and

Brenna Ryan Ellis

CONTENTS

ACKNOWLEDGMENTS

I would like to thank Richard Fleck, friend and mentor, for inspiring me to undertake this project and for encouraging it along the way. I am also very grateful to the Department of English at Hope College for making its resources available in the final preparation of the manuscript. In particular, my sincere thanks to Myra Kohsel for the many hours and talents she contributed to the project at a very busy time. My appreciation also goes to Kelly Jacobsma and Libby Bocks at Hope College, Sara S. Hodson, Curator of Literary Manuscripts at the Huntington Library, Jennifer A. Watts, Associate Curator of Photographs at the Huntington Library, Linda Lewis at Zimmerman Library of the University of New Mexico, and Melody Graulich at the University of New Hampshire. As always, thanks and love to Brenna, Isaac, and Daniel, for their friendship and support.

Mary Hunter Austin might have seen it as the right hat in the wrong place. Harrison Fisher's cover painting for the February 1913 issue of *The Ladies' Home Journal* depicts a carefully sophisticated, stylishly intelligent "ideal woman," already so confident and successful — what does she need with the vote? On *Harper's Weekly* or *The Nation* the painting might have been the image of Austin's considerably more progressive notion of the Young Woman Citizen. She wears a fur, holds a small dog, and her dark hair is topped with a huge and billowing green hat. With her fantastic hats as much a lifelong trademark as her Paiute wickiup writing office and her confident and expansive prose, it was a hat that Austin might have worn.

But for Austin — feminist, nature writer, regional theorist, and social commentator, then at the height of her own career as a magazine writer — the rest of the magazine was something of a fortunate flop. It had "failed to retard in the slightest degree," Austin wrote in 1922, "the successful development of all the ideas it opposed — suffrage, women's clubs, family limitation and the like, — which went on progressively among the very women on whose living room tables the 'Journal' was periodically displayed."[1] It was in this successful current of ideas that Austin made her contribution, not adorning the covers of America's magazines, but rather, like a growing number of influential women writers after the turn of the century, helping to fill their pages with the insights arising from the exciting and evolving role women were making for themselves in American society and culture.

Still best known for her 1903 *The Land of Little Rain*, acknowledged as a classic within the tradition of American nature writing, Austin has been identified, perhaps too specifically, with that tradition. Although much of her work, on a variety of topics, can be read as grounded in her close observations of the natural environment and her sense of living within what she calls the "Earth Horizon," her writing extends well beyond the first-person nature narrative in a rich life's work including fiction, drama, poetry, autobiography, and essays addressing topics pertaining to American and international politics, mysticism and religion, feminism, literary theory, and even automatic writing. In addition to some thirty-four books, praised by Joseph Conrad and H. G. Wells, Austin produced about 250 shorter pieces for the magazines and literary journals of her day. Writing for the periodical market, Austin certainly gained a more immediate, and perhaps a more widespread, recognition and following than she did with her books. Her friend Jack London, who by his own account "never read serials," wrote to Austin in 1915 that he "turned always" to hers.[2] Yet in spite of Austin's popularity and currency during her lifetime, more recent readers have found her magazine essays only through the slow work of hunting piecemeal in library stacks, often among discontinued journals.

This volume, *Beyond Borders*, is the first collection of her nonfiction journalism. The title is intended to suggest both the range of Austin's personal interests and the broad scope of her professional life as she wrote, by her own admission, to satisfy a lively market for magazine copy, and to pay the bills. In her descriptions of the desert in books like *The Land of Little Rain* and *The Land of Journeys' Ending*, Austin captures the unique geophysical character and rhythms of the arid American West. Her self-defined "country of lost borders" (the distant horizon east of the Sierra Nevada, the Owens Valley, the Panamint and Amargosa Mountains of Death Valley, the Mojave, the Funeral Mountains of Nevada) Austin reveals as a geophysical and a literary landscape made borderless by the engagement of the human mind with the spare desert environment. Similarly, when we look at Austin's far-ranging magazine writing as it moves from California to New York, from Santa Fe to London, and across many prominent public issues of the first third of the twentieth century, the sense of borders or limitation disappears altogether, and both Austin's range and the depth of her grounding in the American West are vividly displayed.

Although *The Land of Little Rain* remained in print after its initial publication, most of Austin's extensive and varied work received very little attention after her death in 1934. The exceptions are two critical biographical works by T. M. Pearce, *The Beloved House* (1940) and *Mary Hunter Austin* (1965). The 1969 reissue of *The Basket Woman* (1904) and the 1970 reissue of *The American Rhythm* (1923) signaled Austin's rediscovery as part of a renaissance of interest in both women writers and regional and ethnic studies. Since then, reissues of Austin's nonfiction works *The Land of Journeys' Ending* (1924) and *The Young Woman Citizen* (1981), her autobiography *Earth Horizon* (1932), the novels *Isidro* (1905) and *A Woman of Genius* (1912), and the short story collection *Lost Borders* (1909) have encouraged an overdue appreciation for this original and vital voice in American letters, as have the recent publications of the novella *Cactus Thorn* (1988) and a collection of short fiction *Western Trails* (1987), both edited by Melody Graulich. In addition, two new biographies — Augusta Fink's *I-Mary: A Biography of Mary Austin* (1983) and Esther Lanigan Stineman's *Mary Austin: Song of a Maverick* (1989) — have been written, and Peggy Pond Church's *Wind's Trail: The Early Life of Mary Austin* (1990) has been reissued. Finally, mention should be made of T. M. Pearce's *Literary America 1903–1934: The Mary Austin Letters* (1979), largely a collection of letters written *to* Austin by literary celebrities of her era. This volume continues the ongoing work of making Austin's writing available again to a wider reading audience.

Austin's was the era when the Chautauqua and the highbrow journal tussled, each by its own lights, for the right to uplift the American spirit and intellect. Dismissing the Chautauqua for its superficiality, for simply purveying to its public the "pleasing illusion of actually having what they had only heard about," Austin found an important platform for her thinking in the growing periodical market.[3] It was a medium for which she was much better suited than she is often given credit for as a western writer or author of nature essays. Categorical and theatrical, sometimes intimidating and controversial, Austin was a farsighted and original thinker who wrote and spoke with a clear, personally felt, and authoritative voice and who had the stomach to, as she called it, "sell" her work to a sometimes resistant, almost exclusively male, editorial audience. "So now *The Nation*,

The Bookman, The Freeman and *The Dial*," she once told Mabel Dodge Luhan, "are all captives of my bow and spear."[4]

Austin's writing about the West makes explicit that her vision was rooted in her sense of the western American landscape and her desire for practical and ethical human adaptation to it, not simply as a utilitarian means of survival but concurrently as a spiritual process of discovery. Just as importantly, however, Austin's work demonstrates her commitment to articulating what she described as "Woman Thought," a model for social change meant to be a balancing corrective to what she saw as a narrow and "androcentric culture."[5] Several of Austin's fictional female characters, such as Walking Woman and Basket Woman in the short stories of the same names and her several Paiute *chiseras*, or medicine women, combine these two impulses toward the land and toward honest, unconstrained female selfhood in a single personification. It is also a combination expressed in her nonfiction journalism as well. Austin believed that women must stop thinking of magazines as "the sort of thing Daddy brings home from his hunting"[6] and begin to see them as vehicles for their own expression, for the forward turn, as she called it, that a growing self-confidence among women would bring to American life.[7]

Outwardly self-reliant and confident of her own abilities, Austin rarely hesitated to express her opinions, and the vigor and reputation of her writing as well as the energy of her personality brought her in contact with an astonishing range of individuals. When she moved to New York in 1910, notices in the *Bookman* frequently kept tabs on her activities and movements as she traveled and lectured on literature, women's rights, and Indian reform. In 1915, Henry Ford asked Austin, along with other well-known public figures, to sail for Europe with his unfortunate Peace Ship delegation, an invitation she wisely declined. She named among her acquaintances and correspondents influential women and men in the arts, journalism, social policy, and government, and she was active among the exciting and germinal women and men of the self-styled bohemian circles of Carmel, Greenwich Village, and Santa Fe. Her correspondence, much of which is preserved today in the Mary Austin Collection at the

Henry E. Huntington Library in San Marino, California, reads like an annotated index of those shaping the American cultural scene through the 1920s, including Ina Coolbrith, Charles Fletcher Lummis, Lincoln Steffens, Jack and Charmian London, Herbert Hoover, Edgar Lee Masters, H. G. Wells, Fannie Hurst, Van Wyck Brooks, Andy Adams, Sinclair Lewis, Carl Van Doren, Ruth St. Denis, Amy Lowell, Mabel Dodge Luhan, Sherwood Anderson, Marianne Moore, H. L. Mencken, Willa Cather, Vachel Linday, Ansel Adams, Ezra Pound, Diego Rivera, Robinson and Una Jeffers, and Eugene Manlove Rhodes.

The underlying economics of Mary Austin's association with magazine writing begins with a short history of the venue. With the model of the page-turning dime novel already firmly established by the end of the Civil War, the lively and uncertain American magazine market for which Austin eventually wrote began to boom in the last two decades of the nineteenth century. The *North American Review* and *Harper's New Monthly Magazine* were already prestigious fixtures of literary America, and the second *Dial* added to the range in 1880. But increasingly, public education provided a broader magazine reading clientele. Current affairs journals like the *New Republic* brought a week's perspective to the sensational daily news peddled by the *New York Journal* and the *World*. In 1888, *National Geographic* began to bring the developments of science into the home.

Cheap postal rates for periodicals went into effect in 1879. Mass production methods and new photoengraving processes resulted in more appealing layouts and illustrations at shrinking costs. In addition, ongoing price wars brought the cost of even the genteel magazines like *Harper's* and *Scribner's* nearer the cover prices of the cheap weeklies and miscellanies, and new magazines like S. S. McClure's *McClure's Magazine*, John Brisben Walker's *Cosmopolitan*, and Frank A. Munsey's *Munsey's Magazine* came to an expanding popular market at fifteen cents and under. Lower prices brought more readers and the introduction of increasingly large-scale advertising. This in turn made it possible for publishers to sell a magazine, like a newspaper, for less than it cost to produce it. *Good Housekeeping* developed into a showcase for consumer products, and specialty magazines like *Bicycling World* began to cater to the latest trends. the *Saturday Evening Post* became the literary organ of an expanding business culture, and *Vogue* celebrated material success. By 1900, magazine publishing had completely outgrown its roots, providing light entertainment for the leisure class and becoming a lucrative industry. It was a deadline-driven literary climate that Mary Austin felt willing to explore. "When about 1900 I began to seriously devote myself to a writing career," she recalled later, "I made a list of magazines for which I meant to write in the order of their literary excellence, with *The Atlantic Monthly* at the top."[8]

After publishing in the *Atlantic, Century Magazine, Harper's,* and *Munsey's,* Austin cultivated more specialized markets for her commentary on public life after her move to New York. The peak of Austin's career as a periodical writer came in the 1920s. This was a period of retrenchment for American liberalism and its progressive agenda of optimism, compromise, and reform that had flourished in the Wilson era before the war and that had spawned a thriving reading audience for the great liberal journals of the day. In spite of the disappointment occasioned by the failure of Wilsonian internationalism and the perceived ascendancy of a business culture, *The Nation* and the *New Republic* continued as platforms for the vigorous critique of Babbitts and the "booboisie" that the nation's self-appointed intelligentsia and progressive social commentators continued to voice as counterpoint to a decade overwhelmingly flavored by Republican politics, Rotarian commercial values, and "one hundred percent" Americanism. The literary "new America" of the *Dial,* the announced humanism of the *Forum* and the *Bookman,* H. L. Mencken's catalog of democratic ills in the *Smart Set* and later the *American Mercury,* the enduring optimism and progressive liberalism of *The Nation,* and the motto of the *New Republic* that "the final argument against cannon is ideas" all added their specific idiom to the great rhetoric of national self-consciousness and debate that defined the ground of published liberalism during the 1920s.

Chronologically, Mary Hunter Austin and the modern American magazine grew up together. When Austin was born in Carlinville, Illinois, northeast of St. Louis, on 9 September 1868, Bret Harte was producing the first numbers of the *Overland Monthly* in San Francisco. On the east coast, *Harper's Bazar* had been in publication barely a year. *Scribner's* was two years away.

Austin was the daughter of Captain George Hunter and Susannah Savilla (Graham) Hunter. George Hunter was a lawyer and Civil War veteran who loved books. He nurtured Austin's early love for reading and encouraged the poetry she began writing by age seven. As a child, Austin read her father's first editions of Keats and Shelley, Ruskin, as well as such American writers as Poe, Melville, Hawthorne, Longfellow, and Emerson. In 1870, the family moved outside of town to a house on several acres of land. Austin grew up exploring the gardens, orchards, and bottomlands of this rural neighborhood, and it was there, Austin relates in her autobiography, that beneath a walnut tree at the age of five, she had her first mystical experience of nature, sensing for the first time what she would throughout her life variously call the Voice or Presence that became both a source of consolation and power for her. Austin attended rural schools and after her father's death in 1878, she attended and graduated from small Presbyterian Blackburn College in Carlinville, where she edited her college journal, was elected "Class Poet," and reportedly gained her lifelong habit of wearing extravagant hats, once referred to by one of her friends as "museum pieces of the Victorian age adapted from time to time to meet some notable modern trend."[9] Feeling emotionally spurned by her mother and often overwhelmed by her older brother's narrow and authoritarian role as head of the family, Austin grew up awkwardly, focused inwardly on her own mental and spiritual resources. She developed a dual sense of self that would last her entire life, coming to see herself as two persons, a "Mary-by-Herself" who lived and worked in an often inhospitable world and the more private "I-Mary" of her creative imagination.

After graduating from Blackburn in 1888, without, as she puts it, "a thumbprint of predilection" for choosing a career,[10] Austin was persuaded to move with her mother and older brother to the Tejon district at the southern end of the San Joaquin Valley, not far from Bakersfield, where they optimistically filed claims on homestead land. The ill-conceived farming scheme on three tracts of high desert land was from the beginning a demoralizing failure, and to support herself and her family, Mary found a position teaching in the Kern County public schools. Yet Austin grew in the Tejon. The stark desert environment and the Paiute Indians inhabiting it made more concrete the transcendental mingling of the physical and mental worlds she had learned from Emerson and experienced firsthand herself as a young child. The desert gave her a subject matter and a mode of perception that launched and guided her entire writing career.

In 1891, Austin married Stafford Austin, a luckless vinyardist and gentleman farmer, scion of a wealthy California family. She accompanied him to the farming town of Independence in the Owens Valley, east of the Sierra Nevada Mountains, where he had undertaken to manage a land and irrigation development project diverting water from the Owens River. Her husband's business affairs were not a success, and while their debts mounted, Austin repeated her mother's financial struggle, keeping the family afloat by running a boarding house and teaching school. Her only child, Ruth, was born on 30 October 1892, a physically beautiful child who only gradually began to show the signs of mental retardation.

As she struggled to earn a living and care for her child, Austin was also writing. Accompanying her husband on business trips to San Francisco, Austin met poet Ina Coolbrith, consultant for the *Overland Monthly* and member of the famous San Francisco circle that included such writers as Bret Harte, Joaquin Miller, and Henry George. Austin's earliest published piece, "One Hundred Miles on Horseback," a narrative of her arrival at the family homestead in the Tejon in 1888, had been published in 1889 in Blackburn College's literary magazine, the *Blackburnian*, as the work of its former editor. But Austin's first real success as a writer came in 1892 when her short story, "The Mother of Felipe," appeared in the *Overland Monthly*. Her experiences in the Tejon and in the Owens Valley formed the basis for her early work, stories and sketches that by 1897 quickly began to appear in the *Overland Monthly, Cosmopolitan, Out West, St. Nicholas,* the *Atlantic Monthly,* and *Munsey's Magazine.* Austin's early publications index the young writer's growing personal and professional independence and confidence. She had resumed her teaching in 1895. Frustrated with the family's always tenuous financial circumstances, she separated from her husband in 1896 and in 1897 moved with her daughter Ruth to take up a teaching position at the State Normal School in Los Angeles. In 1900, the estranged parents finally made the difficult decision to place Ruth under care in a private home and later, after the financial success of *The Land of Little Rain* made it possible, in an institution in Santa Clara, where she died in 1918.

While in Los Angeles in 1899, Austin met Charles F. Lummis, editor of *Out West* magazine and author of such books as *A New Mexico David* (1891) and *The Land of Poco Tiempo* (1893). A friend of archaeologist Adolph Bandelier, author of *The Delight Makers* (1890), a romantic novel about the ancient Anasazi of New Mexico, Lummis incorporated his experiences living among Pueblo Indians and Hispanics in New Mexico and other indigenous ethnic material into his own writing. Lummis introduced Austin to his artistic and literary circle, which included poets Sharlott Hall and Edwin Markham, Charlotte Perkins Stetson (later Gilman), and David Starr Jordan, the first president of Stanford University. While Eve Lummis provided friendship to Austin, her husband was a playful and challenging literary mentor and model, often chiding Austin for everything from her style and her errors in Spanish to her seriousness, once inviting Austin to a party by charging her with "the High Misdemeanor of 'not knowing an old California good time when you see it.' "[11]

After a series of Austin's sketches about California and the Great Basin appeared in the *Atlantic Monthly* in 1902 and 1903, Houghton Mifflin agreed to publish them in book form in 1903 under the title *The Land of Little Rain*. Austin's small volume was in the tradition of Thoreau's *Walden* and Muir's *The Mountains of California* and anticipated Leopold's *A Sand County Almanac*. A loosely structured collection of sketches revealing the western environment Austin knew as a landscape of overlapping physical and mental actualities, *The Land of Little Rain* uses Austin's understanding of solitude in conjunction with the observations of other "indwellers" of the western deserts to move from a position outside of place toward an understanding of the individual's involvement in it — a movement from isolation and simplicity to participation and complexity. "A land of lost rivers," she calls the arid West, "with little in it to love; yet a land that once visited must be come back to inevitably. If it were not so there would be little told of it."[12]

Already something of a literary celebrity and a financial success after the publication of *The Land of Little Rain*, Austin was in San Francisco during the earthquake of 1906, contributing her account of the disaster to David Starr Jordan's *The California Earthquake of 1906*. Her acquaintance with Lummis began a lifelong series of associations with loose-knit groups of writers and artists. Between 1904 and 1911, Austin spent time at the Carmel art colony frequented by a self-styled bohemian group including Ambrose Bierce, George Sterling, Jack London, James Hopper, Upton Sinclair, Lincoln Steffens, Robinson Jeffers, and sometimes faculty members of the newly founded Stanford University. John Muir visited frequently. In 1905, Austin built a house in Carmel, five miles south of Monterey. In association with the literati of Carmel, Austin's temperamental penchant for creative and extravagant gestures was for the first time fully released. While still in Independence, she had named the corner of her house where she wrote her "wickiup," referring to the traditional pole and brush lodges of the Paiute Indians of the Great Basin. Behind her new house in Carmel, metaphor became architecture when Austin built an actual wickiup and moved her writing desk into its atmosphere of legend, tradition, and simplicity.

Between 1907 and 1910, Austin lived in Europe, visiting again in 1922. Following the path of Bret Harte, Joaquin Miller, and Mark Twain to London, she quickly gained a reputation there as the first important woman writer from the American West. Hosted by Lou and Herbert Hoover, she met Bernard Shaw, Hilaire Belloc, H. G. Wells, Joseph Conrad, Henry James, and William Butler Yeats, who, she said, told her he never read American books.[13] She participated in several suffragist parades with Anne Martin in London and lectured before the Fabian Society.

Although she briefly returned to Carmel to continue her writing, Austin gave way in 1910 to the persistent cultural tug of New

York City, where she hoped to gain easier access to publishers and the lecture circuit. On 27 February 1911, New York's New Theater staged her play *The Arrow Maker*, directed by George Foster Platt, focusing on the character of a mystical and powerful Paiute *chisera* or medicine woman whose downfall comes as the result of love, and poet and Carmel visitor Charlotte Hoffman began to address Austin in her letters as "Dear Chisera," a habit Austin encouraged. In 1912, Austin moved to New York, where she would live until 1923 and where, in Greenwich Village, she joined the salon company of Mabel Dodge Luhan, whom she would later follow to New Mexico. By 1912, Austin had fully entered feminist causes with such notable reformers as Gilman, Anna Howard Shaw, Elizabeth Gurley Flynn, Margaret Sanger, and Anne Martin. During the World War, Austin worked on the Mayor's Committee for National Defense and later with her friend Herbert Hoover for the United States Food Administration.

Austin had a complex and ambivalent feeling for New York City. Although drawn to its opportunity, she claimed to resent its influence. Although she said she was "bothered by the rage for success,"[14] Austin drove herself to succeed, entering her most rigorous and productive period of writing for periodicals and publishing nine books, including four novels: *A Woman of Genius* (1912), *The Lovely Lady* (1913), *The Ford* (1917), and *No. 26 Jayne Street* (1920). She also published a psychological biography of Christ, *The Man Jesus* (1915), collections of short stories and Native American songs, and her still controversial *The American Rhythm* (1924), an argument for the origins of poetry in the perception of movement in the natural environment.

This level of creative production increasingly made New York seem insulated and narrow, and in 1918, Austin accepted the suggestion of Mabel Dodge to visit Santa Fe, New Mexico. In 1923, she moved there permanently and, through the network of Dodge's newly transplanted Taos circle, spent time with Witter Bynner and Alice Corbin Henderson and with such visitors as Ansel Adams, Willa Cather, Vachel Lindsay, Sinclair Lewis, and briefly, D. H. Lawrence. In the Southwest, Austin discovered the legacy of the Anasazi and the rich textures of Pueblo and Hispanic cultures that would surface in her later work, such as *The*

Land of Journeys' Ending, and that would animate her political involvement with the causes of Native Americans. She worked with activist John Collier of the American Indian Defense Association to protect the integrity of Pueblo land holdings and helped organize the Indian Arts Fund to support traditional Native American artists. In 1925, she built the adobe *Casa Querida* in Santa Fe on the El Camino del Monte Sol, a winding dirt road known for its writers' and artists' studios scattered throughout the chamisa, sagebrush, and piñon pines. The final years of her life she spent there, finishing ten more books, including her often beautiful and telling autobiography, *Earth Horizon*. Five days before her death on 13 August 1934, when Alice Corbin Henderson organized a "poet's roundup," Austin was introduced as "for years the boss of the crowd."[15]

With the inescapable presence and authority of the land, as well as its imaginative and material appropriation, involved so intimately with the history, mythology, and ongoing public life of Americans, it should be no surprise that American nature writers have seldom been in any sense only nature writers. Austin is an important case in point. In *The Land of Journeys' Ending*, Austin explains:

> Man is not himself only. . . . He is all that he sees; all that flows to him from a thousand sources, half noted, or noted not at all except by some sense that lies too deep for naming. He is the land, the lift of its mountain lines, the reach of its valleys; his is the rhythm of its seasonal processions, the involution and variation of its vegetal patterns. If there is in the country of his abiding, no more than a single refluent color, such as the veiled green of sage-brush or the splendid wine of sunset spilled along the Sangre de Cristo, he takes it in and gives it forth again in directions and occasions least suspected by himself, as a manner, as music, as a prevailing tone of thought.[16]

Austin's suggestion that the experience of the natural world grounds all human cultural practices and finds expression in human thought and creativity seemingly far removed from the local concerns of place and environment gives important insight, not only into her own diverse work, but also into the entire tradition of American nature writing. Writing about the natural world of America in terms of the wild, the primitive, and the mystically understood, has been like the education of Rousseau's Emile — the mandate "follow nature" has also meant leaving the garden and journeying in the world of human affairs, a search for an ideal society and state. Thoreau's *Walden* is a microcosm of this phenomenon. For Thoreau, going to the woods to live deliberately is a political and rhetorical event created by its own public announcement. Furthermore, the mental experience of wildness, and "plain living and high thinking" in its midst, provided Thoreau with what he called his "Realometer,"[17] a handy psychic device that can easily be taken along on sojourns from the pond for the purpose of evaluating human behavior in the world beyond the woods.

Thoreau's metaphor of the Realometer gives us an important tool for understanding the work of Mary Austin. More than any major American nature writer since Emerson, Austin represents a diversity of concerns. While it would be a mistake to invent for Austin's work a totalizing thematic consistency, it would also be equally off the track to say that nature, or more specifically the western environment of which she so wonderfully and usefully wrote, was simply one of Austin's interests, one topic competing with others in an active and pluralistic mind. For Austin, such concerns as women's rights, economics, regional identity, international affairs, and Native American thought and cultural survival were founded on her fundamentally spiritual, phenomenological experience of nature and her determination to voice her distinctively, self-consciously female perspective on that experience.

To all issues she took on, Austin brought the Realometer she built from these sources. Austin's novels, for example, superficially as romantic in some ways as the fiction of Mary Hallock Foote or as influenced by the local color impulse as those of Gertrude Atherton, whom Austin considered something of a rival, embody within their narrative real social issues, dramatizing important economic and gender concerns, the latter a theme that surfaces most prominently in the novels of her New York period like *A Woman of Genius* (1912), depicting a heroine modeled on herself, and *No. 26 Jayne Street* (1920). In *Earth Horizon*, Austin relates that after he read her 1906 novel *The Flock*, President Theodore Roosevelt sent a forestry expert to interview her to see if the novel's claims regarding the mismanagement of government lands were based in fact.

Austin's extensive involvement in public affairs was part of the background to her writing. Even in the year before her death, she was an active supporter of Diego Rivera in his dispute with the Rockefellers over the content of the artist's commissioned Radio City murals. In addition to her campaigning for suffrage, Native American rights, and legal reform, and her work setting up community kitchens and food planning during the war (the August 1917 *New York Worker* carried a picture of Austin and a crowd of hoe-carrying boys headed off to work in a war garden in New York's Van Cortlandt Park), Austin was also active in water and land management issues. When Austin first saw Los Angeles in 1888, she described it as "daunted by the wrack of the lately 'busted' boom,"[18] a city whose streets were marked out by surveyor's stakes and lined with dying palm trees. By 1900, however, the city had a population of 100,000, and by 1904, that figure had doubled. Austin actively resisted the efforts of the Los Angeles Department of Water and Power under the predatory William Mulholland to gain control of the Owens River for the growing city. Already in 1904 something of a minor celebrity after the publication of *The Land of Little Rain*, Austin managed to land an audience with Mulholland in Los Angeles. After the interview, Mulholland is said to have remarked, "By God, that woman is the only one who has brains enough to see where this is going."[19] In 1927, she was appointed to the Seven States Conference empaneled to consider the construction of what would be Hoover Dam and Lake Mead. Austin bucked the general spirit of boosterism that animated the conference by arguing against the project. "None of us will live to see that *debacle*," she writes.[20]

Austin's determination to write developed shortly after her graduation from Blackburn. From the beginning, writing was difficult and frustrating, and her work was persistently interrupted by the fortunes of marriage, motherhood, and economic constraint, as well as by the sense of inadequacy many an apprentice writer feels. Austin, for one, calls it "that very real and heartrending anguish of the creative worker."[21] Susannah Hunter, who unaccountably held Austin responsible for Ruth's retardation, also refused to recognize her daughter's writing, reportedly remarking that Austin's stories were "beyond me,"[22] a comment Austin never accepted from a mother she knew to be an intelligent observer of current women's issues.

During her entire career, Austin thought of herself as a woman who wrote for a living. The memory of her mother faced with what Austin called "the strange indignities offered to widowhood" remained with her.[23] So did a keen sense of the limited financial opportunities available to single women, a situation that may have prompted her own unhappy marriage. Austin began her career at a time when writing was not considered an altogether respectable profession for a woman anyway, and even as a successful writer, she seldom made enough in royalties from her books to live on. As a result, Austin increasingly turned to the magazine market to supplement her income. In fact, writing magazine essays became a large part of what she saw in 1922 as "the rather sordid struggle of my literary life,"[24] and she sometimes referred to herself as a hack writer, forced by financial needs to write on subjects that did not always interest her. When she moved to New York City, she did so in great part to gain better access to outlets for her publications and lectures, and once there, she sold articles by tirelessly soliciting editors, often making personal visits to their offices to promote projects. In spite of these efforts, the work was difficult. The 2,500-word essays she preferred to write, because they paid better, were often difficult to come by, and her life in the city was characterized by frequent moves in search of less expensive apartments. "This problem of living in New York grows more difficult every year," she wrote her friend Daniel MacDougal in 1922 as her novel *No. 26 Jayne Street* proved a financial failure.[25] Similarly, her autobiography is clear in its picture of publishing as a business and writing as a livelihood. Referring to a series of pieces on the life of a woman writer, Austin remarks, "I sold them cheaply on the understanding that eventually I was to be remunerated when 'Harper's Weekly' got into a paying vein, which it never did."[26]

In spite of these problems, Austin professes in *Earth Horizon* "The thing I suffered from worst in New York was boredom. The people I met were seldom interested in the things that interested me." [27] Yet Austin worked to satisfy their demand for reading materials, while maintaining the integrity of her own ideas. Austin's personal financial position, occasioned in part by the sociological situation of women on either side of the turn of the century does not fully explain the existence, to say nothing of the range, particular themes, nor incisiveness of her magazine essays. After all, some women writers active during the period wrote antifeminist pieces. Some promoted Republican "dollar diplomacy," investment and industrial development in South America. Even so, Peter Wild writes that "as an intellectual woman she was by necessity a rebel,"[28] and in her magazine writing, this impulse mingles with the financial motive. She sometimes celebrated the success of her convictions. "I told them exactly where to get off so far as the rest of the world was concerned," she wrote Mabel Dodge in 1920, "and all but the *New Republic* group and Mencken and the *Smart Set* rushed over to my side."[29]

As Austin's reputation grew in the years following her move to New York, the nature of the obstacles she faced became more clearly defined for her. In *Earth Horizon*, Austin remembers:

> Along in the middle of my writing career, when I was still struggling with the New Theater, I had more than a little trouble with editors and publishers. There was a far-reaching idea in most editorial offices that writers were dancers, posturing at the editorial dictation. There were more than a few magazines that had no other idea than to wave their writers back and forth; one, two, three, turn; four, five, six, turn. I have a notion that more than a little of it came of the indisposition of women writers to be so directed; the unwillingness of men editors to step out of their way. There was a growing interest

in the experience of women, as women, and a marked disposition of men to determine what should and should not be
written."[30]

Although Austin had established herself as a talented short
story writer, poet, and author of nature essays, this reputation
only grudgingly yielded her a platform to comment on a broader
range of issues. Part of Austin's own specific "trouble with editors" arose from their recognition and identification of her as a
writer on the natural environment. As much as it reflects Austin's
preoccupation with the American West, her consistent emphasis
on the region also signals her editors' use of her talents as an acknowledged western storyteller and expert on things western.

Unfortunately, this kind of recognition at times masked an
unwillingness to acknowledge the scope of her interests or the
range of the issues she, as a woman, was competent to undertake.
In 1922, Austin observed: "It is disconcerting then, to discover,
after the removal of the political bar, that in everything but the
personal accomplishment we are still in a state of practical nullity toward our national culture."[31] Largely in response to her
feminism, many editors and critics were much more comfortable
when Austin confined herself to her "personal accomplishment,"
nature writing, and stayed safely beyond the somehow more serious male worlds of politics and the arts. Even John Farrar, one
of Austin's more supportive editors, suggests this in a 1923 *Bookman* sketch. "Hers is, to be sure," Farrar explains, "a mind made
to the desert's order."[32] Like that of Hardy, London, and Conrad,
Farrar argues, Austin's thinking and artistic expression had been
permanently shaped by the natural landscape and human presence of a specific place. "Mary Austin went into the southwest
and the desert made her life articulate. It has never failed her
since nor freed her. She has never fruitfully forsaken its mastery
and she never can."[33]

Farrar is correct as far as that goes, but what he misses is the
operation of the Realometer, the influence of Austin's perception
of nature and adaptation in virtually all her writing. She "makes
a mess of many little matters," Farrar writes, by following "con-

science or the guidance of the momentary into more personable ways,"[34] a not-so-subtle code for the domain of political, economic, and artistic life certain types of New York male culture brokers tended to see as their own special province. Van Wyck Brooks, who more strenuously resented Austin's mysticism and feminism and who tended to trivialize regional concerns, was adamant in his insistence that Austin ought to be sequestered from addressing the broader affairs of the nation, criticizing her for a failure to "establish a real relation with the world beyond the desert."[35]

What Brooks may have chosen to ignore is that the relation was already in place, nurtured in the ideological context that fostered both Austin's nature writing and the mingling currents of American liberalism before and after World War I. Austin's notions about the overlapping necessity and aesthetic value of progressive human adaptation to the environment can be situated in the larger development of evolutionary biology, process psychology, and pragmatic philosophy occurring during her lifetime and, as a result, in the liberal theories of progress that assumed that humans were slowly, steadily, moving toward a safer, saner, and better society.

The appearance of "A Land of Little Rain" in 1903 coincides with the publication of John Dewey's *Studies in Logical Theory* and the beginning of the Chicago School of philosophy, an important benchmark in the articulation of instrumentalist philosophy as it would serve both socialist and progressive liberal social theory well through the 1920s. The tools of close observation and inductive exposition that Austin employed in her descriptions and interpretations of western landscapes and indigenous peoples, amateur ecology and ethnography as they might be, speak to the liberal faith in "facts" and the scientific method as debunkers of superstition and agents of progress, just as her emphasis on adaptation parallels then current progressive social theory.

In her detailed imagery of the Mojave desert, Anasazi ruins, or Pueblo ritual, Austin's affinity for liberal ideology might have been overlooked, or seen as the determinism of local color, particularly by critical readers intent on viewing America's hinterlands as a rustic cultural wilderness and the urban cosmopolitan East as the arbiter of all progressive values. Austin's persistent suggestion that Native American worldviews and practices have a message for modern Euro-America would have been particularly easy to marginalize within her recognition as a regional writer.

But in spite of the editorial obstacles she so enjoyed describing, the fact remains that Austin found a ready audience for her periodical essays, those pertaining to the West as well as those that did not. Beneath the apparent irony of this welcome reception, Austin's career suggests that we question the scope and impact, if not the vociferousness, of the liberal prejudice against the rural, the local, and the natural. Further, it affirms what the presence in New Mexico of Mabel Dodge Luhan, D. H. Lawrence, and other writers and artists makes plain — that Austin's Southwest registered more as a category of the exotic than as a territory of the hinterlands. For educated liberal readers, as for novelists and artists, it was just too far west of the tasteless, colorless, and much denigrated Midwest to symbolize philistinism in quite the same way. In any case, the range of Austin's essays indicates that her work resides more centrally within the ideology and rhetoric of American liberalism than might at first be supposed, and we can speculate that this, too, accounted for a measure of her popularity as a periodical writer.

Particularly after her move to New York in 1910, Austin used her magazine work as a vehicle to take what the desert taught her into that "world beyond." She taught her female readers to resist being confined anywhere, perhaps especially within the tempting ghetto of their own recognized and sanctioned talents, excluded from a somehow more significant, more authentic male world of ideas and actions. Her journalism is the literature of what she called the "spotlight." She developed this metaphor in one of her most widely read books, her 1923 *Everyman's Genius*, itself arising from a ten-part series of *Bookman* articles she had written for John Farrar during 1923 and 1924 entitled "Making the Most of Your Genius." Echoing the circular imagery of her notion of the Earth Horizon, Austin defines the spotlight as "the normal circle of immediate attention."[36] With Austin's magazine writing, this perceptional spotlight resulted in a risky, conspicuous, and contemporary body of often occasional work. As is always the case with such work, it is vulnerable to criticism on the grounds of literary quality or political persuasion. It does, however, reveal a woman writer typecast as western and hence, by the prevailing mode of accounting, doubly limited, willing to engage patriarchal assumptions and a mainstream eastern establishment with her own original, independent, and polemical point of view.

In *The Land of Journeys' Ending*, Austin observes that modern Americans "go about with a vast impedimenta of Things, clanking on trails of our Frankenstein culture."[37] What these essays make clear is that Austin's journalism records a messy and sometimes costly process of taking up that impedimenta of public life and turning it into an expression of the "thousand sources" that infuse the human heart with spirit. Her magazine Realometer was often enough well tuned and incisive and spoke from a perspective she describes as both a place, her "Sacred Middle," and as a female perception, her "Woman Thought." *Beyond Borders* is an occasion to listen to the voice that arose from that careful balance.

NOTES

1. Mary Austin, "Women as Audience," *Bookman* 55 (1922): 2.

2. Jack London to Mary Austin, 1915, qtd. in T. M. Pearce, ed., *Literary America, 1903–1934: The Mary Austin Letters* (Westport, Conn.: Greenwood, 1976), 75.

3. Mary Austin, "The Town That Doesn't Want a Chautauqua," *New Republic* 47 (1926): 195.

4. Mary Austin to Mabel Dodge Luhan, 28 Sept. 1920, Luhan Collection, Beinecke Rare Book and Manuscript Library, Yale University.

5. Austin, "Women as Audience," 1.

6. Austin, "Women as Audience," 3.

7. Mary Austin, "The Forward Turn," *Nation* 125 (1927): 59.

8. Mary Austin, "How I Learned to Read and Write," in *My First Publication*, ed. James D. Hart (San Francisco: Book Club of California, 1961), 63.

9. Qtd. in T. M. Pearce, ed., *Mary Hunter Austin* (New York: Twayne, 1965), 26.

10. Mary Austin, qtd. in Pearce, *Austin*, 25.

11. Charles F. Lummis, qtd. in Pearce, *Literary America*, 23.

12. Mary Austin, *The Land of Little Rain* (1903; reprint, New York: Anchor-Doubleday, 1962), 5.

13. William Butler Yeats, qtd. in Pearce, *Austin*, 40.

14. Mary Austin, *Earth Horizon: An Autobiography* (1932; reprint, Albuquerque: Univ. of New Mexico Press, 1991), 330.

15. Alice Corbin Henderson, qtd. in Helen MacKnight Doyle, *Mary Austin: Woman of Genius* (New York: Gotham, 1939), 284.

16. Mary Austin, *The Land of Journeys' Ending* (1924; reprint, Tucson: Univ. of Arizona Press, 1983), 437.

17. Henry David Thoreau, *Walden, or Life in the Woods and On the Duty of Civil Disobedience* (New York: Signet-NAL, 1960), 33.

18. Austin, *Earth Horizon*, 186.

19. William Mulholland, qtd. in Marc Reisner, *Cadillac Desert: The American West and Its Disappearing Water* (1986; reprint, New York: Penguin, 1987), 82.

20. Austin, *Earth Horizon*, 363.

21. Austin, *Earth Horizon*, 269.

22. Austin, *Earth Horizon*, 255.

23. Austin, *Earth Horizon*, 91.

24. Mary Austin to Daniel MacDougal, 10 May 1922, Mary Austin Collection, Henry E. Huntington Library, San Marino, Calif.

25. Austin to MacDougal, 10 May 1922.

26. Austin, *Earth Horizon*, 319–20.

27. Austin, *Earth Horizon*, 330.

28. Peter Wild, *Pioneer Conservationists of Western America* (Missoula: Mountain, 1979), 82.

29. Austin to Luhan, 28 Sept. 1920.

30. Austin, *Earth Horizon*, 319.

31. Austin, "Women as Audience," 1.

32. John Farrar, "The Literary Spotlight; 22: Mary Austin," *Bookman* 53 (1923): 47.

33. Farrar, "Literary Spotlight," 47.

34. Farrar, "Literary Spotlight," 51.

35. Van Wyck Brooks and Otto L. Bettmann, *Our Literary Heritage* (New York: Dutton, 1956), 218.

36. Mary Austin, *Everyman's Genius* (Indianapolis: Bobbs Merrill, 1925), n.p.

37. Austin, *The Land of Journeys' Ending*, 345.

Beyond Borders

"I will spare you mercifully all quotations,"[1] *Austin writes of her first contributions as "Class Poet" to her college literary journal, the* Blackburnian, *for which she served as editor. Still, it was to this familiar publication that Austin sent her first serious work, the narrative essay "One Hundred Miles on Horseback," an account of the last leg of her family's journey to the Tejon country of the San Joaquin Valley of California. While it prefigures in its close observation* The Land of Little Rain *that would follow fourteen years later, "One Hundred Miles" is plainly more tentative, the novel impressions of a younger person encountering the strangeness of a new place. In this regard, it invites comparison to the diary records of other nineteenth-century westering women, such as Phoebe Judson and Sarah Royce. The essay conveys a sense of incipience and expectation, as well as a perception of California as shaped by literary renderings, such as the stories of Bret Harte and the romantic tones of Helen Hunt Jackson's* Ramona, *an image of California Austin would later eschew. Austin ends enticingly with the promise that the story of "the wild and romantic delights of the life of a pioneer" will be continued at another time.*

One Hundred Miles on Horseback

Those whose lives have been spent in the prairie lands of Illinois can have little conception of the pleasure of a journey on horseback through the most picturesque part of California.

To us, wearied with two thousand miles of hot and dusty railroad travel, and two days and nights of anguish in a Pacific coast steamer the prospect was delightful beyond comparison.

The point of starting was the "boom stricken" city of Pasadena, the point to be reached lay in the southern extremity of the San Joaquin valley, one hundred miles to the north. Between the two points rose three mountain ranges with their out-lying foothills and intervening valleys.

Our outfit including the saddle horse and white topped "prairie schooner" drawn by a team of sturdy bronchos, appurtenances of the "mover" would have done credit to a Pike county Missourian.

Leaving Pasadena at noon we passed northward, through the most beautiful portion of the city, out toward the suburban town of Garvanza in the Eagle Rock valley. A drizzling rain, forerunner of the rainy season, compelled me to abandon my equestrian ambitions and make an inglorious retreat to the canvas shelter of the wagon. In this fashion we completed the afternoon journey through the Eagle Rock valley, one of the many similar valleys opening out on the southern slope of the Sierra Madre mountains.

The valley is populous and fertile, rich in vineyards and orchards. The peach and apricot orchards were shedding their dull leaves, with only here and there a touch of gold or crimson where a breath of frost from the mountains had reached them. An autumn landscape in California is strangely devoid of color, and this silent succumbing to a process of nature made us homesick for the glory of the October hills of Illinois.

Published in the *Blackburnian* (1889) and in *One Hundred Miles on Horseback*, ed. Donald P. Ringler (Los Angeles: Dawson's Book Shop, 1963). Reprinted by permission of Muir Dawson.

The second day's journey lay through the San Fernando valley, so named by the founders of the old Spanish mission of San Fernando

Brown and sere the fields look now after the abundant harvest of barley and oats has been garnered. Thousands of sheep and cattle feed on the surrounding foot hills and the sight of the outlandish looking Mexican shepherds with their flocks and faithful dogs recalled vividly well-known scriptural scenes and places. Alternating with the fertile strips were long, stony stretches, marking the "wash" of some mountain stream, and covered with brown tangled "chapparal," bristling with the dried stalks of the species of the yucca known as the "Spanish Bayonet."

Many of the stalks reach the height of fifteen or twenty feet and in the spring are crowned with hundreds of fragrant wax-like blossoms.

These stony places are the favorite haunts of the prickly pear, and here they raised their impenetrable barriers on every side. We gathered some of the rich purple fruit and found it not unpleasant to the taste, very much of the flavor of watermelon, but slightly more acid.

Here as elsewhere in California we noticed the absence of singing birds. The shrill pipe of the quail or the whirring wings of the chapparal cock were the only sounds that broke the silence. An occasional jack rabbit familiarly known as the "narrow gauge mule" hops across the road solemnly flapping an ear as a mute protest at our intrusion.

In the fertile portions of the valley we were much interested in the curious homes of the ground squirrel. They live in communities, the color of their fur varying according to the color of the soil they inhabit.

The valley was entirely treeless except that in some few well watered regions the willow and live oak flourished. We "foraged" in the large vineyards for which the valley is famous, but with indifferent success, for the first crops had been converted into wine or raisins, and the second growth was inferior in size and flavor.

We passed the second night at San Fernando. Although noted in local papers as a growing city, San Fernando is but a small village of some two or three hundred buildings, chief among which are an immense hotel, (vacant) and a new Methodist Theological Seminary in the first year of its existence.

The old mission of San Fernando is situated some two or three miles from the town, and is probably one of the best preserved missions in the state.

Starting at sunrise the next morning, our road followed the line of the railroad over the foothills into the mouth of the San Fernando pass. Soon after entering the hills the two roads separate, the railroad passing through the range by means of a tunnel, while the wagon road goes over the summit.

For a short distance the road rises gently, following the windings of a mountain stream, then suddenly the ascent becomes steep and the canyon walls narrow to within a few feet of the wheel track.

We passed over the summit without accident and found the descent on the other side comparatively easy. The north side of the mountains is usually heavily wooded with live oaks, willow, sycamore and higher up a few straggling pines.

A day's journey in front of us lay the second range of the Sierra Madre or "mother mountains" lifting their bare wind-swept peaks and wrinkled sides without a break, as far as the eye could see, and behind lay the range just crossed, apparently as impassable. The remainder of the day's travel alternated well cultivated fields and wooded pasture lands with long stretches of sand. Frequently we were obliged to give the right of way to the fierce looking Mexican shepherds and their flocks. Stopping at Newhall for supplies we saw two Mexican hunters bringing in half a dozen deer for shipment to the Los Angeles markets.

We camped that night at the first bit of natural green grass we had seen in California. It is known as salt grass and is found in the neighborhood of alkali springs. It has a decidedly salty taste and resembles what is known at home as "goose grass."

Growing about the spring we found the round, green "tule" reeds. Those who have read *Ramona* will remember that it was in a hut thatched with these reeds that she and Alexandre began their housekeeping. During that night the coyotes came close up to the camp and howled, and growled, and barked, and shrieked like so many demons. There seems to be no limit to the hideous noises these animals can produce.

About nine o'clock next morning we entered the mouth of the San Francisquito canyon. The canyon walls rose higher and narrower as we proceeded, sometimes swelling gently until the hills were rounded to a perfect dome, covered with grease-wood and enlivened by the dark red satin smooth stems, and olive green foliage of the manjanita; sometimes bare and ragged cliffs with strata turned, and twisted, and folded back upon itself, bearing on its face the marks of primeval fire and flood.

It is not possible for the mind to conceive of a force that could throw the elements of the solid earth into such confusion as is here displayed.

Opening out of the main canyon are innumerable smaller cross-canyons. In each one of these some Mexican or Indian has built his hut of adobe or tule, planted his grape-vine and set up his hive of bees. The houses are low and thatched, ornamented with strings of red pepper and skins of wild animals fastened on the walls of the house to dry, and all overflowing with dogs and children in dirty but picturesque confusion. Occasionally, somewhat back from the house a little white wooden cross gleaming over a mound of earth made pathetically human a scene that might have been disgusting or merely amusing.

The greater part of the honey shipped from California comes from the San Francisquito canyon.

All along the canyon we saw traces of the gold seekers.

About the middle of the afternoon we began the ascent of what is known as the long grade. The canyon becomes so narrow that there is no room for a wagon road at the bottom, consequently the road is forced to climb the side of the mountains. For a distance of two miles it rises gradually, winding about the side of the mountain while far below it the stream rushes and roars and tumbles, flashing in tiny cascades or foaming in angry eddies. Up, up the road winds, a yellow line along the steep slope of the canyon wall, every curve apparently terminating in a sheer precipice, but the point being reached behold on the rounded front of the next hill the road lies far above. It rises in this spiral line from the bottom of the canyon to a point one thousand feet above, where looking up one can see only blue sky pierced by peaks more deeply blue, and down the almost vertical wall of the canyon one can scarcely see the tops of the tall trees that hide the brawling stream.

There is something indescribably awesome, traveling thus in the fast deepening twilight through these narrow gorges where the mountains close in upon us so silently and mysteriously that one unfamiliar with such scenes would declare that there is no outlet in either direction.

On previous nights the petticoated members of our party had camped in the wagon, but to-night, wrapped in our blankets, Indian fashion, we lay peacefully down under the bright stars of California in the shadow of her majestic mountains and — snored.

The next day being Sunday we rested a part of the day, but owing to the difficulty of finding suitable camping places, were obliged to break camp about three o'clock in the afternoon.

The ascent known at the Tejunga Pass is long and steep and on account of the altitude and the lateness of the hour the air was quite chilly, but the summit once reached we were fully repaid for our pains. Below us lay the green panorama of the canyon, while round about us peak after peak rose into view, violet, purple, and rose, outlined against the flaming gold of the sunset sky. The whole arch of the heavens was suffused with glowing rose color save where the ridge on which we stood intercepted the waning light, leaving a broad band of deepest blue along the eastern horizon, where the stars were already gleaming.

On the next to the last day of our journey we took dinner at "Hell," a supply station and hostelry, known sometimes as "Gorman's," situated just at the head of the valley. Bob McCord, from Nova Scotia, familiarly known as "Old Three-finger," one of the *habitues* of the place, a miner, a veritable "forty-niner," looking as if he had just stepped out of one of Bret Harte's stories was there on a periodical "drunk." He was very urgent in his entreaties for the man of our family to "come take one more drink and swear off."

The Tejon canyon, through which the remainder of the journey lay, is very beautiful. Never have I seen such magnificent trees as the live oaks that crowded each other in the canyon and on the hills. Festoons of grapevines hung from the willows across the noisy stream and heavy garlands of mistletoe dropped from the branches of oak and sycamore.

On the afternoon of the eighth day we came out on the north side of the Tehachapi mountains in the valley of the San Joaquin. Here it is that I write, here where the tarantulas sun themselves on our front porch, the owls hoot on our roof at night, and gray coyotes come trotting up under our very windows. The mountains curve about us from east to west, and below us on the slope we can catch the blue gleam of a lake. Scarcely a day or night but some member of the family calls us to "come and look;" sometimes at some new glory of cloud and sun on the mountains, sometimes at a herd of antelope feeding close to the house, or an eagle cleaving the air with swift wings, or the red light of an engine climbing down the long slope of the mountains thirty miles away; or at some freak of the sense-deceiving mirage that makes flowing rivers or still lakes where yesterday was dry land.

We are twenty-five miles from town, but only seven miles from the famous Tejon ranch, where the oranges are now getting ripe and yellow and the olives purpling under the December sun.

But time and space compel me to postpone even the merest mention of the wild and romantic delights of the life of a pioneer in the "pampas" of the San Joaquin until some better opportunity.

NOTE

1. *Earth Horizon* (1932; reprint, Albuquerque: Univ. of New Mexico Press, 1991), 167.

"*I have been here several months at the edge of the deserts and have found your books. They have been such a relief to me after all the other books of the western country I have read. What Twain and Hart missed you have found.*"[1] So Sherwood Anderson wrote Austin from Berkeley in 1923. What Austin found was initially set forth in her first widely recognized essay about the California desert. "A Land of Little Rain" appeared in the Atlantic in 1903 as one installment in a series of essays that would be collected and published by Houghton Mifflin later the same year with a few changes as The Land of Little Rain, the book that launched Austin's writing career.

The same issue of the Atlantic also contains Frederick Jackson Turner's essay "Contributions of the West to American Democracy," in which the historian elaborates on his then famous "frontier thesis," arguing that "the frontier regions have exercised a steady influence toward democracy."[2] While Austin might have agreed with that assertion, as far as it goes, she would have objected to the sense of finality and certainly to the Eurocentrism in Turner's observation that by 1890 "the first rough conquest of the wilderness is accomplished."[3] "A Land of Little Rain" speaks to Austin's sense of what she saw as a very much ongoing process of human acquaintance with the West. In Austin's view, human interaction with the "frontier" of the arid western environment is governed by the need for a kind of human adaptation that she elevates to the level of an ideal "ecological" value, an essential mode of accommodation and harmonization expressed in aesthetic perception, political economy, biological and social evolution, and most importantly, spiritual growth. Drawing heavily on the model of Native American adaptation to the environment, Austin's sense of successful life in a constrained environment is both retrospective and actively prospective. Placing her entire life's work within this dynamic framework, Austin concludes: "My books have no sequence other than the continuity of the search for the norm of moral and spiritual adjustments which I have tried herein to describe."[4] It is in the context of this sense of process that Austin's remark in the following essay "not the law, but the land sets the limit" is best understood.

A Land of Little Rain

East away from the Sierras, south from Panamint and Amargosa, east and south many an uncounted mile, is the Country of Lost Borders.

Ute, Paiute, Mojave, and Shoshone inhabit its frontiers, and as far into the heart of it as a man dare go. Not the law, but the land sets the limit. Desert is the name it wears upon the maps, but the Indian's is the better word. Desert is a loose term to indicate lands that support no man; whether the lands can be bitted and broken to that purpose is not proven. Void of life it never is, however dry the air and villainous the soil.

This is the nature of that country. There are hills, rounded, blunt, burned, squeezed up out of chaos, chrome and vermilion painted, aspiring to the snowline. Between the hills lie high level-looking plains full of intolerable sun glare, or narrow valleys drowned in a blue haze. The hill surface is streaked with ash drift and black, unweathered lava flows. After rains water accumulates in the hollows of small closed valleys, and, evaporating, leaves hard dry levels of pure desertness that get the local name of dry lakes. When the mountains are high and the rains heavy the pool is never quite dry, but dark and bitter, rimmed about with the efflorescence of alkaline deposits. A thin crust of it lies along the marsh over the vegetating area, which has neither beauty nor freshness. In the broad wastes open to the wind the sand drifts in hummocks about the stubby shrubs, and between them the soil shows saline traces. The sculpture of the hills here is more wind than water work, though the quick storms do sometimes scar them past many a year's redeeming. In all the Western desert edges there are essays in miniature at the famed, terrible Grand Canyon, to which, if you keep on long enough in this country, you will come at last.

Since this is a hill country one expects to find springs, but not to depend upon them; for when found they are often brackish

As first published in the *Atlantic Monthly* 91 (1903). Reprinted by permission of the School of American Research.

and unwholesome, or maddening, slow dribbles in a thirsty soil. Here you find the hot sink of Death Valley, or high rolling districts where the air has always a tang of frost. Here are the long heavy winds and breathless calms on the tilted mesas where dust devils dance, whirling up into a wide, pale sky. Here you have no rain when all the earth cries for it, or quick downpours called cloud bursts for violence. A land of lost rivers, with little in it to love; yet a land that once visited must be come back to inevitably. If it were not so there would be little told of it.

This is the country of three seasons. From June on to November it lies hot, still, and unbearable, sick with violent unrelieving storms; then on until April, chill, quiescent, drinking its scant rain and scanter snows; from April to the hot season again, blossoming, radiant, and seductive. These months are only approximate; later or earlier the rain-laden wind may drift up the water gate of the Colorado from the Gulf, and the land sets its seasons by the rain.

The desert floras shame us with their cheerful adaptations to the seasonal limitations. Their whole duty is to flower and fruit, and they do hardly, or with tropical luxuriance, as the rain admits. It is recorded in the report of the Death Valley expedition that after a year of abundant rains, on the Colorado desert was found a specimen of Amaranthus ten feet high. A year later the same species in the same place matured in the drought at four inches. One hopes the land may breed like qualities in her human offspring, not tritely to "try," but to do. Seldom does the desert herb attain the full stature of the type. Extreme aridity and extreme altitude have the same dwarfing effect, so that we find in the high Sierras and in Death Valley related species in miniature that reach a comely growth in mean temperatures. Very fertile are the desert plants in expedients to prevent evaporation, turning their foliage edgewise toward the sun, growing silky hairs, exuding viscid gum. The wind, which has a long sweep, harries and helps them. It rolls up dunes about the stocky stems, encompassing and protective, and above the dunes, which may be, as with the mesquite, three times as high as a man, the blossoming twigs flourish and bear fruit.

There are many areas in the desert where drinkable water lies within a few feet of the surface, indicated by the mesquite and the bunch grass (*Sporobolus airoides*). It is this nearness of unimagined help that makes the tragedy of desert deaths. It is related that the final breakdown of that hapless party that gave Death Valley its forbidding name occurred in a locality where shallow wells would have saved them. But how were they to know that? Properly equipped it is possible to go safely across that ghastly sink, yet every year it takes its toll of death, and yet men find there sun-dried mummies of whom no trace or recollection is preserved. To underestimate one's thirst, to pass a given landmark to the right or left, to find a dry spring where one looked for running water — there is not help for any of these things.

Along springs and sunken water-courses one is surprised to find such water-loving plants as grow widely in moist ground, but the true desert breeds its own kind, each in its particular habitat. The angle of the slope, the frontage of a hill, the structure of the soil determines the plant. South-looking hills are nearly bare, and the treeline higher here by a thousand feet. Cañons running east and west will have one wall naked and one clothed. Around dry lakes and marshes the herbage preserves a set and orderly arrangement. Most species have well-defined areas of growth, the best index the voiceless land can give the traveler of his whereabouts.

If you have any doubt about it, know that the desert begins with the creosote. This immortal shrub spreads down into Death Valley and up to the timber-line, odorous and medicinal as you might guess from the name, wandlike, with shiny fretted foliage. Its vivid green is grateful to the eye in a wilderness of gray and greenish white shrubs. In the spring it exudes a resinous gum which the Indians of those parts know how to use with pulverized rock for cementing arrow points to shafts. Trust Indians not to miss any virtues of the plant world!

Nothing the desert produces expresses it better than the unhappy growth of the tree yuccas. Tormented, thin forests of it stalk drearily in the high mesas, particularly in that triangular slip that fans out eastward from the meeting of the Sierras and coastwise hills where the first swings across the southern end of the San Joaquin Valley. The yucca bustles with bayonet-pointed leaves, dull green, growing shaggy with age, tipped with panicles of fetid greenish bloom. After death, which is slow, the ghostly hollow network of its woody skeleton, with hardly power to rot, makes the moonlight fearful. Before the yucca has come to flower, while yet its bloom is a creamy cone-shaped bud, of the size of a small cabbage full of sugary sap, the Indians twist it deftly out of its fence of daggers and roast it for their own delectation. So it is that in those parts where man inhabits one sees young plants of *Yucca aborensis* infrequently. Other yuccas, cacti, low herbs, a thousand sorts, one finds journeying east form the coastwise hills. There is neither poverty of soil nor species to account for the sparseness of desert growth, but simply that each plant requires more room. So much earth must be preempted to extract so much moisture. The real struggle for existence, the real brain of the plant, is underground; above there is room for a rounded perfect growth. In Death Valley, reputed the very core of desolation, are nearly two hundred identified species.

Above the treeline which is also the snowline, mapped out abruptly by the sun, one finds spreading growth of piñon, juniper, branched nearly to the ground, lilac and sage, and scattering white pines.

There is no special preponderance of self-fertilized or wind-fertilized plants, but everywhere the demand for and evidence of insect life. Now where there are seeds and insects there will be birds and small mammals, and where these are, will come the slinking, sharp-toothed kind that prey on them. Go as far as you dare in the heart of a lonely land, you cannot go so far that life and death are not before you. Painted lizards slip in and out of rock crevices, and pant on the white hot sands. Birds, humming-birds even, nest in the cactus scrub; woodpeckers befriend the demoniac yuccas; out of the stark, treeless waste rings the music of the night-singing mocking-bird. If it be summer and the sun well down, there will be a burrowing owl to call. Strange, furry, tricksy things dart across the open places, or sit motionless in the conning towers of the creosote. The poet may have "named all the birds without a gun," but not the fair-footed, ground-inhabiting, furtive, small folk of the rainless regions. They are too many and too swift; how many you would not believe without seeing the footprint tracings in the sand. They are nearly all night workers, finding the days too hot and white. In mid-desert where there are not cattle, there are no birds of carrion, but if you go far in that direction the chances are that you will find yourself shadowed by their tilted wings. Nothing so large as a man can move unspied upon in that country, and they know well how the land deals with strangers. There are hints to be had here of the way in which a land forces new habits on its dwellers. The quick increase of suns at the end of spring sometimes overtakes birds in their nesting and effects a reversal of the ordinary manner of incubation. It becomes necessary to keep eggs cool rather than warm. One hot, stifling spring in the Little Antelope I had occasion to pass and repass frequently the nest of a pair of meadow larks, located unhappily in the shelter of a very slender weed. I never caught them setting except near night, but at midday they stood, or drooped above it, half fainting with pitifully parted bills, between their treasure and the sun. Sometimes both of them together with wings spread and half lifted continued a spot of shade in a temperature that constrained me at last in a fellow feeling to spare them a bit of canvas for permanent shelter.

There was a fence in that country shutting in a cattle range, and along its fifteen miles of posts one could be sure of finding a bird or two in every strip of shadow; sometimes the sparrow and the hawk, with wings trailed and beaks parted, drooping in the white truce of noon.

If one is inclined to wonder at first how so many dwellers came to be in the loneliest land that ever came out of God's hands, what they do there and why stay, one does not wonder so much after having lived there. None other than this long brown land lays such a hold on the affections. The rainbow hills, the tender bluish mists, the luminous radiance of the spring, have the lotus charm. They trick the sense of time, so that once inhabiting there you always mean to go away without quite realizing that you have not done it. Men who have lived there, miners and cattle-men, will tell you this, not so fluently, but emphatically, cursing the land and going back to it. For one thing there is the divinest, cleanest air to be breathed anywhere in God's world. Some day the world will understand that, and the little oases on the windy tops of hills will harbor for healing its ailing, house weary broods. There is promise there of great wealth in ores and earths, which is no wealth by reason of being so far removed from water and workable conditions, but men are bewitched by it and tempted to try the impossible.

You should hear Salty Williams tell how he used to drive eighteen and twenty mule teams from the borax marsh to Mojave, ninety miles, with the trail wagon full of water barrels. Hot days the mules would go so mad for drink that the clank of the water bucket set them into an uproar of hideous, maimed noises, and a tangle of harness chains, while Salty would sit on the high seat with the sun glare heavy in his eyes, dealing out curses of pacification in a level, uninterested voice until the clamor fell off from sheer exhaustion. There was a line of shallow graves along that road; they used to count on dropping a man or two of every new gang of coolies brought out in the hot season. But when he lost his swamper, smitten without warning at the noon halt, Salty quit his job; he said it was "too durn hot." The swamper he buried by the way with stones upon him to keep the coyotes from digging him up, and seven years later I read the penciled lines on the pine headboard, still bright and unweathered.

The palpable sense of mystery in the desert air breeds fables, chiefly of lost treasure. Somewhere within its stark borders, if one believes report, is a hill strewn with nuggets; one seamed with virgin silver; an old clayey water bed where Indians scooped up earth to make cooking pots and shaped them reeking with grains of pure gold. Old miners drifting about the desert edges, weathered into the semblance of the tawny hills, will tell you tales like these convincingly. After a little sojourn in that land you will believe them on their own account. It is a question whether it is not better to be bitten by the little horned snake of the desert that goes sidewise and strikes without coiling, than by the tradition of a lost mine.

For all the toll the desert takes of a man it gives compensations, deep breaths, deep sleep, and the communion of the stars. It comes upon one with new force in the pauses of the night that the Chaldeans were a desert-bred people. It is hard to escape the sense of mastery as the stars move in the wide clear heavens to risings and settings unobscured. They look large and near and palpitant; as if they moved on some stately service not needful to declare. Wheeling to their stations in the sky they make the poor world-fret of no account. Of no account you who lie out there watching, nor the lean coyote that stands off in the scrub from you and howls and howls.

NOTES

1. Qtd. in T. M. Pearce, *Literary America, 1903–1934: The Mary Austin Letters* (Westport, Conn.: Greenwood, 1976), 177.

2. *Atlantic Monthly* 91 (1903): 83–92.

3. 83.

4. *Earth Horizon* (1932; reprint, Albuquerque: Univ. of New Mexico Press, 1991), 367.

Austin cultivated and thoroughly enjoyed the friendships of quite a number of famous men, including Charles Fletcher Lummis, George Sterling, Jack London, Herbert Hoover, and H. G. Wells. Austin writes that at the Carmel artists' colony in 1905 Sterling and London were "the first men I had known who could get drunk joyously in the presence of women whom they respected."[1] Calling him "someone to whom the actualities of conduct were more important than opinion about it,"[2] Austin found her relationship with H. G. Wells, whom she visited while in London in 1909 and again in 1922, of a somewhat more dignified character.

Wells had read and publicly praised Austin's work, but when she talked literature with Wells on a walk on Hampstead Heath, while Wells was in the middle of an ongoing dispute with the Fabians, she was warned by her friend Herbert Hoover that, as Austin tells it, "I might have to choose between Mr. Wells and my other friends."[3] Austin, as might be expected, made no such choice. Even when American critics turned against Wells for his persistent enthusiasm for a liberal theory of progress in The Outline of History, labeling him "the last of the Great Parlor Socialists,"[4] Austin supported him, although when Wells turned prophetic, she did allow that "something, the humor and elan that had characterized his earlier novels, was gone out of him."[5]

"An Appreciation of H. G. Wells, Novelist" is Austin's introduction to Wells's new novel, Marriage, which was shortly to be serialized in the American Magazine. In her introduction, Austin recognizes Wells's modernity, socialist inclinations, and feminism, although she suggests that some of his female characters may know him better than he does them.

from An Appreciation of H. G. Wells, Novelist

The very ancient conception of a genius as one seized upon by the waiting Powers for the purpose of rendering themselves intelligible to men has its most modern exemplar in the person of Herbert George Wells, a maker of amazing books. It is impossible to call Mr. Wells a novelist, for up to this time the bulk of his work has not been novels; and scarcely accurate to call him a sociologist, since most of his social science is delivered in the form of fiction.

There are people who call him a Socialist, and that, with some definition, is what Mr. Wells calls himself; there are others who call him a revolutionist; but, under whatever caption, he is distinguishedly a maker of books, informing, vitalizing, indispensable books; and when one attempts to account for the range and variety of Mr. Wells' product, the first inescapable inference is that behind them is a man of broad and specific learning.

It is not possible, by naming the schools where he has been educated, to give any notion to an American audience of the quality of Mr. Wells' scholarship. He is not, as we understand it, a University man, but so far as his learning relates him to his time, better educated than most University men dare profess to be — a scholar of human conditions. Chiefly, besides finding out how the things that are came to be, Mr. Wells' preparation for his work consists in living.

He has lived, not episodically nor by proxy, as so many literary men tend to do, but consciously and actively, for forty odd years. How many American men one knows who let their wives and children do half their living for them! But Mr. Wells has done his own living, which probably accounts for his having done so much of his own thinking. At any rate he has never clouded his genius with the obscurations of an "Art Atmosphere."

At the time I knew Mr. Wells in London I never persuaded him to speak but once of Art.

Originally published in the *American Magazine* 72 (1911). Reprinted by permission of the School of American Research.

"An artist," said he, "has nothing to do with success; neither must he concern himself whether he is read by one or one million; he must just do his work." And Mr. Wells has demonstrated that, if an artist does that sincerely, success will have much to do with him.

The first book of Mr. Wells to attract attention in America, though it was not his first writing, was "The War of the Worlds," published in 1898, the first of a group of singular but irresistible romances in which Mr. Wells, by anticipating the bent of scientific discovery, or by deflecting it slightly from its present course, created an original background against which he worked out the socialistic remedy for the economic disorder.

It was just here that the Powers seized upon Mr. Wells. The pressure of economic discontent in England, so much greater than the home-bred American can realize, the chafing of regenerative forces against the social superstitions (conservatism is the stately word for it, but really there is a lot of it on a par with the objection to sitting down with thirteen at table) produced the electrical conditions which demanded a man as the medium of discharge. No doubt Mr. Wells was primarily a novelist, but then and for a long time the social forces were too much for him. All through his earlier work the artist can be seen shaken in the teeth of the Social Consciousness. Even in his latest work, "The New Machiavelli," it runs neck and neck with the story until the reader is left a little in doubt which of the two had the better of it. But in 1900 Mr. Wells wrote "Love and Mr. Lewisham," and gave the first intimation of what his work might become when he had subordinated the reforming impulse to the simple mastery of human life. "Love and Mr. Lewisham" is the story of a very usual young man and the struggle of his ambitions and egoisms with the mating instinct. It is so satisfying as a story that it is not until a long while after reading it you discover that what Mr. Wells has been saying all the time is that it is only our disordered social system that sets the mating instinct at war with a man's personal development. The real trouble with Mr. Lewisham was not that he was in love or ambitious, but that he found it difficult to make a living. That, in one way or another, is the crying difficulty of Young England, and none sees more clearly than Mr. Wells the relation of all our so-called immoralities to the economic condition and the impossibilities of remedying one without correcting the other.

Socialism is Mr. Wells' remedy, but it must be understood that his particular brand of it is not so much a system as a state of mind; a kind of awareness, a realization of the pain of social maladjustment in the farthest, least little toe of the social organization. Earlier in his career Mr. Wells was active in the society of Fabians, and the various tentative measures by which the growing pains of social discontent manifested. But of the theory of Socialism as it exists now in England he says, "It has gone up into the clouds and the practice of it into the drains." Those who are interested can find the best explication of Socialism as it appeals to Mr. Wells as a "plain human enterprise" in "The Misery of Boots," first published as a Fabian tract. It is impossible to avoid the conclusion, on reading it, that you are some kind of Socialist yourself. . . .

NOTES

1. "George Sterling at Carmel," *American Mercury* 11 May 1927: 69.
2. *Earth Horizon* (1932; reprint, Albuquerque: Univ. of New Mexico Press, 1991), 311.
3. *Earth Horizon*, 311.
4. Qtd. in Frederick J. Hoffman, *The 20s* (1949; reprint, New York: Free Press-Macmillan, 1962), 388.
5. *Earth Horizon*, 343.

Standard features of the popular magazines and journals in which Austin published her work during and immediately after World War I were short articles, pictorial segments, and advertisements focusing on the role that American women had in the war effort. A wartime American Telephone and Telegraph Company advertisement, for example, shows the image of a female telephone operator visually linking background scenes of factories, rail yards, and marching troops. "Applied Patriotism," the heading reads. A generation before Rosy the Riveter, women were represented as what one Sunset photo item called "Amazons in overalls," or elsewhere as patriotic scab workers filling in for striking male unionists, and frequently as loyal brides left behind. "A war honeymoon in overalls," reads a caption for a photograph of a woman railroad worker in Tacoma.

As a committed and active feminist and suffragist during the era preceding the extension of the franchise, Mary Austin recognized the importance of the war, sometimes in spite of the representations of women in print, in softening the constraints of rigid gender roles for both women and men. In her 1919 The Young Woman Citizen and in such essays as "Woman and Her War Loot" and "Sex Emancipation Through War," Austin comments on how the widespread participation of women in the war effort accelerated the process of expanding female influence in American public life. In "Woman and Her War Loot," she writes:

> It is the fact that this war is the only war in which women, as women merely undistinguished by class or country, have gained anything. Suddenly after two hundred and fifty thousand years of militarism, they find themselves as a sex emerging from war with a share of the loot as well as the losses. In this unprecedented situation, men, who have not invariably made the best use of their own battle gains, are asking one another, and women are asking themselves, what they are to do with it.[1]

Austin's alliterative loot/losses distinction, commodifying the results of the war, suggests the fundamentally economic focus of her analysis, yet Austin freely acknowledges the limitations of merely economic gain and predicts in the following essay that "some of the freedom gained by this war will have to be surrendered at the end of it."

Sex Emancipation Through War

The Day the Most American writer came home from the front, I asked him what he thought it would all come to.

"Well," he hesitated, "I don't know that I can tell you until I have been home and talked it over with my wife."

"If you have to do that," I insisted, "talk it over with your wife, I mean, then I know what you think."

"I guess you do," he soberly agreed, and when we had talked it over between us, that proved to be the case.

What this war will come to is the thing the world has needed more than anything else, more than Religion, though it will help to bring religion back; more than Democracy, though it is in its way a democratic phase; more than Civilization, though there can be no civilization without it. It will come to sex emancipation. It is so certain to come to this that it is probably perfectly safe to say that the war will not end until we are emancipated from sex, and anything we can accomplish toward that emancipation will have its share in bringing the war to an end.

Notice I say WE. We are in the habit of thinking that it is women only who are in need of sex emancipation. As a matter of fact, it is only women who are clever enough to know that they need it. Men are so wrapped and swaddled and tied into their sex that most of them don't know yet that this is not the natural order of things. They think that the political world is a male place into which women have broken by a not wholly fortunate accident, within which they can only stay by becoming in some fantastic way *un*womanly, *un*sexed. They — the men — are so gorged and saturated with sex, as sex may be expressed in social conditions, that they think of this war as cataclysmic, made in Germany or in Hell, or anywhere except where it actually is, in the very center of male consciousness, and made there only by virtue of our not being able to see it as an exhibition of masculinity run amuck.

Originally published in the *Forum* 59 (1918). Reprinted by permission of the School of American Research.

Get it out of your mind for a moment that sex is a function. Sex is the organizing centre of personality. It is probably the chief difference between a man and a ghost. It is the whole round of the personal complex, with the machinery for perpetuation attached. For man it involves self-expression, combativeness, paternity, protectiveness; for woman, self-immolation, maternity, fostering.

Not to have all of these in some degree is to be undersexed; to have any one of them in excess is to be in need of sex emancipation. Judge for yourself what nations of the earth are at this moment most in need of it.

The world is really a very feminine place, a mother's place, conceptive, brooding, nourishing; a place of infinite patience and infinite elusiveness. It needs to be lived in more or less femininely, and the chief reason why we have never succeeded in being quite at home in it is that our method has been almost exclusively masculine. We have assaulted the earth, ripped out the treasure of its mines, cut down its forests, deflowered its fields and left them sterile for a thousand years. We have lived precisely on the same terms with our fellows, combatively, competitively, geocentrically. Nations have not struggled to make the world a better place, but only to make a more advantageous place in it for themselves. Man invented the State in the key of maleness, with combat for its major occupation, profit the spur and power the prize. This is the pattern of our politics, our economic and our international life, a pattern built not on common *human* traits of human kind, but on dominant sex traits of the male half of society. It is even marked, in certain quarters of the earth, with intrinsic male weaknesses, the strut, the flourish, the chip-on-its-shoulder, the greed of exclusive possessions, the mastery of the seas, the control of world finance.

Three Pet Sex Superstitions

There is no particular reason why the world should be lived in this fashion; no reason in intelligence, I mean, no logical compulsion. Other and more comfortable patterns have often been devised, but the things that tie us to the present are the things that clearly prove the first proposition; — that this war is war for sex emancipation. For we are tied to this androcentric pattern by three pet sex superstitions:

First, the superstition that the work a human being may do in the world is determined by sex.

Second, that the social value of a woman is established by what some man thinks of her.

Finally, that the man alone must "support" the family.

A superstition is a belief persisted in after it has lost all foundation in experience. Even before the war we were beginning to suspect the footlessness of the old idea that Divine Providence had marked out women from the beginning for not more than two or three occupations. The war has come in time to save us endless agonies of doubt and discussion as to whether women have strength enough, or brains enough, for the four hundred and fifty-seven callings which war has added to those already open to women.

We have had so many other tremendous things to think of that many of us have missed the significance of this wholesale, bloodless overthrow of a five-thousand-year-old superstition. When you think what it cost to rid a small portion of the world of the superstition of idol worship, or of hearsay, what tortures and burnings and riving of families, this sudden reversal of ideas about work and women is one of the wonders of civilization.

The basic prejudice against women in the world's work has not been so much against their working as against the conditions of credit and wages. Wherever they could work in the obscurity of their own homes or social unimportance, dull and heavy labors requiring little more than brute strength for their accomplishment actually are performed by women in Europe, and to some extent in America. Cooking for sixteen hay hands in a Mississippi Valley in August is not any more a ladylike occupation than harvesting the hay in Belgium.

CAMOUFLAGE ABOUT WOMAN'S
INTELLECTUAL ACHIEVEMENT

And there has always been a great deal of camouflage about woman's intellectual achievement. When I was last in England I became very well acquainted with a woman whose business it was to furnish speeches for M. P.'s. She collected statistics and historical instances, suggested illustrative anecdotes, figures and apt comparisons. But she used to turn them over typewritten in such a way that, with a good conscience, the M. P. could call them "notes," in deference to the British superstition of male superiority, without which she could never have kept her job. I was also told in France that M. Curie's was not the only laboratory in which the scientific research was done by women, though it was the only one in which the woman scientist had acknowledgment. Things of this kind must have been true to a much greater extent than is generally imagined. Otherwise it would not have been possible for France and England to keep up their advance step on substitute labor, of a kind that was believed, and had believed itself, intrinsically impossible.

The truth is that we have never had any idea how sex-ridden industry is. The first great emancipator was the man who invented the press-the-button method. With the introduction of electrical and other labor-saving devices, human brawn as an element of factory production has been made to take a place second to woman's native faculty for concentrating her attention in seven different directions at once.

The most significant thing that F. R. Still found to report of British labor since the war, was that "in no place was there the lugging, tugging, lifting, pushing, pounding or mauling" which he had formerly seen. For a great majority of operations required in munition factories, physical strength, though indispensable so long as the factories were run by men for men, had been superceded by cranes, levers, trolleys and the like contrivances for utilizing woman's nimbleness and rapidity. The same sort of statement is made by a Chicago manager with five hundred women employees. He says: "Female labor, properly conditioned, is a benefit to the entire shop," and goes on to explain that the necessity of fitting the work to the more delicate female mechanism has led to many improvements in processes and routing and turnovers. In other words, under modern conditions it turns out that the superstition of man's superior strength has clogged the wheels of industry. Men have put more physical force into industry than was necessary, simply because they had it to spend. Labor has used itself up in the interest of a sex distinction for which there is very little call or occasion.

Doubtless, the moment the end of the war is in sight there will be all sorts of hospitals set up for the rehabilitation of disabled social prejudices, but it is impossible to think that there will ever be a return to the "lugging and tugging."

Industry Keyed to Man's Rhythm

One of the most interesting examples of the emancipation of industry from the waste of sex prejudice, comes from Ohio, where it was discovered that woman's instinctive fear of machinery could be turned to account. In an emergency women were put to the management of overhead cranes, these vast and clanking mechanisms which turn the beholder dizzy with their impersonal implacability. Very shortly it was found that the number of accidents was lessened, fewer risks were taken. Just how many lives annually are sacrificed to the male fetish of risk-taking it would be difficult to say. It is quite enough for our purpose to know that the woman operator is sufficiently afraid of the mechanism she handles not to be afraid to stop the machinery when there is a question of risk.

Most interesting of all the revelations made by studies in industrial efficiency of women is the one which relates to the periodic interruption of woman's energy. This has always been a stumbling block for the most enthusiastic advocate of women in industry.

Nobody is so stupid nowadays as not to know that the nation will eventually be the loser in any attempt to disregard and override the potential motherhood of its women. But all our efforts to deal with this factor have been very stupidly based on the notion that man is the norm, and any variation which woman exhibits is a disability. Even in factories where efficiency in production is attained by alternate periods of rest and activity, the whole business has been keyed to man's rhythm. Nobody knows just who first discovered that woman's rhythm was not less effectual, but simply different. I first saw it exemplified in a factory where women were testing steel balls for ball-bearing.

The test was the sense of touch, of the *back* of the hand, if you please, as being more sensitive than the inner surface.

The efficient manager had discovered that better results were attained if the alternation of touch and rest, touch and rest, went to a kind of tune; one two *rest*, one, two, three, *rest*.

That is the germ of the discovery that the chief reason why women fag earlier than men in many kinds of factory work, is that all our factories are speeded and set for men, who seem to get along perfectly on a steady, work, *rest*, work, *rest*, alternation. Change the rhythm of the work to one better suited to the age and sex of the operative, and the output will rise directly.

MAN MORE TIMID AT THE UNTRIED THAN WOMAN

Similar discoveries are being made as to the intellectual fitness of women for work that has always been supposed to belong to men. There are probably ineradicable differences between the aptitudes of men and women, but the war has done much to demonstrate that they are not the traditional distinctions of superior and inferior. There is no difference in the *kind* of aptitude required for handling a telephone switchboard, which is universally conceded to women, and train dispatching, or the work of the "tower women," which railroads are finding it possible to employ.

The difference is one of *quality*, of being able to produce a steady quality of attention for given periods. In other words, it is not so much brains as nervous stability that is required.

Women themselves have always known that "nervousness" in women is not a sex trait. As much of it as is not deliberately produced "for the trade," — since men thinking about women have liked to think of them as timorous — has been the result of woman's forced living in a world which she is permitted to know very little about. Man himself was "nervous" when the world was comparatively an unknown place, likely to see ghosts, hear voices or be frightened into fits by the unexplainable. He is to this day more timid of the untried than woman. That nervous instability in women is part of our camouflage of sex, is shown by the report of the British Health Department, which demonstrates that with all their sorrow and strain, and in spite of their unaccustomed labors — perhaps because of them — the health of the English women has improved during the war. That means that their capacity for work involving nervous tension and responsibility has increased with the demand upon it.

But the nature of many employments thrust into women's hands by the war, has revealed still more the waste of our sex obsession. We move now in the neighborhood of subtle forces, X-rays, Hertzian waves, radioactivity, chemical reaction, — a region in which woman's finer sensibility becomes something more than a substitute instrument. For many such delicate adjustments women are indispensable. It begins to appear that by the exclusive use of maleness we have been trying to dissect our way to the secret of the universe with a spade instead of a scalpel. And right here we are afoul of the oldest, least reasonable of our sex superstitions.

There is no history of the development of the idea that a woman has no value to society except that which man gives her, as the object of his desire and the mother of his children. Like Topsy, it simply "growed" out of man's nature. Men sacrifice themselves to womanhood, its racial function; they sacrifice themselves and the world to their love for a particular woman. But whoever heard of a man putting himself aside because the world needed some woman's gift for architecture, or biology, or sociology, more than it needed *his* contribution. Men have never hesitated to take a woman out of society and insist that every gift, every possible contribution of hers to general human welfare shall be excised, aborted, done with. That is probably why we have to have wars occasionally, and a desperate need of those woman gifts to teach us the crime of such social waste.

THE EFFECT OF THE UNIFORM ON GIRLS

The obsession of the personal in men's customary ways of thinking about women shows in ways little suspected by the men themselves. A Chicago manager of five hundred young women says that he has found uniforming the girls has proved a help in "securing their modesty," and the increased respect of the men workers "not in a moral way," he explains, "but in the mental attitude." What he means is that the uniform enables the men to think of girls not as "the girls," but as workers. A member of the National Council of Defense expressed something of the same thing to me recently. We were talking of women's part in the war, which I thought inadequate.

"But," said he, puzzled, "what work *can* women do in the war?"

"Well, there are eight million or so in the industries — " I reminded him.

"Oh! you mean labor!"

What *he* meant was that those eight or ten million women had, for him, escaped the category of sex. They had been emancipated into labor. When he thought of them as women they were unimportant to the war, but as labor they were indispensable. I should say that three years of this war have set that type of sex emancipation at least a hundred years forward.

At one of these informal conferences of women which nobody ever hears about, but have much to do with determining our place among the nations, we were told of the efforts being made to overcome the industrial prejudice against mature age in women workers.

Women's Period of Industrial Efficiency

It seems that women wage workers go into the discard at thirty-five, ten years younger than men workers, twenty or thirty years younger than professional women. The speaker told how the women begin to break at thirty, after years of speeding up and inadequate feeding and with the fear of dismissal hanging over them, succumb in a few years. She told what was being done to restore the working capacity of those women, their confidence in themselves and hope for the future. "But that," she said, "is only half the story."

"And the other half," we insisted.

Well, the other half proved to be the half-conscious sex prejudice of managers and foremen; the desire to surround themselves with the freshness of youth and youth's flattering docility, unwillingness to pay to older women the deference of experience, undue valuation of the quality of "pep," vague resentment toward wage earning married women, and the dullness of perception exhibited by men generally toward women who make no sex appeal. And naturally the employment of girls leads to the work all being routed and speeded to young rhythm, to the consequent disadvantage of the mature worker.

Some of the freedom gained by this war will have to be surrendered at the end of it, but I think in calculating the returns of peace we underestimate two of the psychological factors. We underestimate the dramatizing effect of war work and the power of the drama to raise the plain of performance. The failure of chivalry between the sexes has been one of the terrors waved by the anti-feminists over every advance of sex emancipation, the fear that women doing work formerly done by men can not claim the feminine exemption. This has always been rather a stupid fear, because it assumes that the attention of chivalry is paid to an attitude, a posture of femininity rather than to a fact. But even where this is the case, the glamour of war adds a touch of heroism to the woman taking a man's place which seems to penetrate even the dullest maleness.

DEFERENCE TO GIRLS IN INDUSTRY

Nothing less favorable to fitness could be thought of than the subway rush-hour crowd. If such a crowd chose to demand of a young woman guard the physical capacity of a man, the young woman would be down and out in the first round.

But a finer democracy waking in the American spirit makes no such demand upon her; chivalry forbears to require her to fight with a weapon which she has not. To see a home-coming crowd defer to a girl conductor because they know that she can't do anything to them is the nicest thing that has happened in America since the war. It would be, if any Prussian could see and understand it, the best guarantee that America knows exactly what she means when she talks about keeping the world safe for Democracy. It means that Americans do not take advantage just because they think they are strong enough to get away with it.

The other force which we underestimate is the effect of the war on men, who through its adventures are released to fundamental male activities.

There seem to be at least three things that men universally and in the nature of things do better than women: exploration of the physical world, invention and poetry. Man is the perpetual adventurer, who by a long process of stupidity has been made over into a kind of social hermaphrodite, a male-mother, whose sole duty and occupation it is to trot back and forth between his job and his offspring with the expected morsel.

Vast numbers of men have been unsexed in this fashion to such a degree that only a war will pry them loose from it. They dare not adventure, do not know how to invent, and are ashamed to sing. If they have moments of rebellion against their fate they cloak it with the duty of "supporting the family" and salve the hurt with the vanity of being the Distributor of Benefits.

Being in this unsexed and inferior state, they require continually to be kept up to their work by large doses of flattery, "inspired," they call it. But no man who is leading a full masculine life needs to be chucked up for it.

Now, there never was any reason in nature or logic why the man should be the sole support of his wife and children; it is just one of those things which has grown up out of the strange human impulse to associate habit with propriety. The natural duty of the individual is to contribute all that is in him to society, and to see that society gives back enough to provide for his offspring. It is utterly unimportant how or through which parent the provision comes. A lot of men are only going to learn this through the adventure of war releasing the mainspring of masculinity. Thousands of desk men and counter men are going to be raised by this war to something like their original male aptitude and capacity. And that is one of the things which is going to make it possible for many of them to accept the idea of their wives in their old jobs. The men aren't going to need a lot of those jobs back; never again. They are going to want something more their size, something more male than ribbon selling or bookkeeping.

You hear the awakened adventurousness of men discussed as one of the hazards of war. It is one of war's advantages. The periods of invention and enterprise which follow on war are due to the new alignment of sex normalities, more women released to conserving, nourishing labors; more men freed to break new ground.

SEX MASTERY, NOT SEX MYSTERY, NEEDED

Of course these gains in the emancipation of industry from sex will have to be consolidated with mastery over some other phases of the relation of men and women. The stability of woman's hold on the work of the world depends on her control of the liability to child-bearing. Maternity must be voluntary; it must not lie forever a hideous uncertainty, to leap out upon her from her most sacred moments. Love must no more threaten with disease and disaster. There must be no more mystery about sex if there is to be mastery.

Toward this the war has helped prodigiously by lifting the taboo on sex intelligence. For the first time Europe has faced the cost in man-power of the Social Evil, it has faced the iniquity of the reproach of illegitimacy. At the end of the war the whole world will have to face the normal demand of women for marriage and children in a world depleted of marriageable men. It is too early to say how that demand will be met.

But it is not too early to say that if that problem forces us at last to look squarely and without superstition at the problem of marriage, it will be worth the cost in husband and children. Governments of the world must prepare themselves, not necessarily to have their women demanding marriage of some sort, but certainly demanding a rational basis for whatever decision is finally reached. If we can never be wholly emancipated from the facts of sex, we can at least emancipate our way of dealing with it.

NOTE

1. *Sunset: The Pacific Monthly* 42 (1919): 13.

Finding the editors of the leading current affairs magazines published in New York "lashed to their publications . . . not willing to accept the idea that there might be anything elsewhere going on,"¹ Austin at times found her interests in Native Americans or the aesthetics and politics of the West somewhat grudgingly welcome. As she accused cosmopolitan New York of its own style of provincialism while living in the city during the early 1920s, ironically Austin, the western regionalist, at times felt herself embattled with a smug Northeastern narrow-mindedness that represented to her the worst of what a regional perspective could be. "New York: Dictator of American Criticism" is an early statement of Austin's belief that the domination by a largely male, New York-based editorial point of view limited the development of a national literature.

Certainly Austin's position has its basis, at least in part, in her seemingly instinctive sense of resentment to what she saw as a highly qualified acceptance by the New York publishing world. Her own reaction to this unfamiliar urban world turned out to be equally cool. She began her life in the city with energetic curiosity, with "an effort to know New York, the face of it, what went on in its streets and neighborhoods, its hours and occasions."² Years later, from the perspective of life in Santa Fe, Austin would write: "New York had failed to engage the exigent interests of my time. It was not simple nor direct enough; bemused by its own complexity . . . it was too much intrigued with its own reactions, took in the general scene, too narrow a sweep."³

In her autobiography, Austin hints at the extent to which her experience of New York was a complex function of gender relations that encompassed both her professional and personal selves. By her account, her interactions with men as she first explored the city predicted the self-preoccupation and fixed ideas she later critiqued in male editors and publishers. Taking odd jobs — typing, arranging flowers, selling shoelaces and pencils — and moving from one cheap room to another, she notes that "no man ever discovered in me anything but the attraction of strangeness, the flattery of interested attention." She concludes: "There were none of them able to make room for me, as a person, however much as a woman I might be desired; and on my part, love was not enough."⁴

Of her move to Santa Fe in 1923, Austin writes: "I could be useful here; and I felt I could get back a consideration from the public that would in a measure make up for the loss of certified ladyhood."⁵

New York: Dictator of American Criticism

Ever since, in 1914, we turned, with a first faint sense of dereliction, an inquiring eye on our national consciousness, there has been a steady output of books about American writing and American thinking. That at least is what one would conclude from a list of the titles. But an examination of the contents of such books proves that the greater number of them are about what a small New York group thinks ought to be written and thought.

Against our hundred million the smallness of the group stands out; the list of authors is shorter than the titles, for in the past six or seven years some of them have found it necessary to express themselves twice. There are a few detached, academic studies from men attached to universities, and the rest are from young New Yorkers, all under forty, in one case under thirty. Evidently there is something in our American temperament which is complaisant to the immature point of view, or we do not take criticism seriously enough to make it worth while for men of mature years to devote their time to it.

And this immaturity of view is apparent not only in the books but in the periodicals devoted primarily to criticism; youth and the pastime of youth, the building up of criteria of criticism in cliques and groups. There is a notable disposition of the critics towards election among themselves, towards the badge and gesture of augury. But even where the groups differentiate, they exhibit a common derivation from New York.

Something more is indicated here than the natural concentration of literary workers around the publishing trade centers. Most of the criticism which rises to book publication has had its turn in London, or even in Paris. But a very little inquiry reveals that its authors have never lived west of Broadway or north of Fifty-ninth. There are even editors of magazines devoted to the development of the literary consciousness in America who have never held it to be an indispensable condition of their work that

Reprinted from *The Nation* magazine, 111 (1920). © The Nation Company, Inc.

they should know something outside of New York. All this, of course, without prejudice; it is simply that nothing outside New York has presented itself to them as being worth knowing.

Under these conditions criticism in America is urban — citified to a degree not approximated by the urbanity of London or Paris. English writers have homes in the country along with the significant members of their audience. Paris is the capital of a homogeneous people. But New York is, in respect to the rest of our country, only a half-way house of immigration, a little less than a half-way house for European thinking. The preponderance of the foreign-born or foreignly derived among our self-constituted literary mentors partly accounts for their detachment from the vast extra-Manhattan territory. Criticism is the natural resort of half knowledge; with an active intelligence and a City College degree one may go far in a milieu which poses a total ignorance of the American process as the best qualification for classifying its product.

Recently in a London journal one of these young critics had fun with the general movement of non-New York American writers to absorb into their work the aboriginal, top layer of literary humus through which characteristically national American literature, if we are ever to have it, must take root. He succeeded in making it appear that it appeared to him ridiculous. But no English critic, supposing one to arise so ignorant of the true processes of national literature, could get space for ridiculing the aboriginal roots of Shakespeare or Yeats. One suspects that the New Yorker is only admitted to the making of an exhibitional ass of himself because it flatters the English concept of our being still a colonial dependency. The point of our departure from such a state would be marked by our ceasing to celebrate half mythical Irish kings in Celtic measures, and by our beginning to handle our American material in generic American metrics.

One wonders what part is played in this schism between literature and the process of nationalization by the preponderance of Jews among our critical writers. There is nothing un-American in being a Jew; it is part of our dearest tradition that no derivation from any race or religion inhibits a contribution to our national whole. We could not without serious loss subtract the Jewish contribution from our science or our economics, or dispense with the services of the younger Jewish publishers. It is only when the Jew attempts the role of interpreter of our American expression that the validity of the racial bias comes into question. Can the Jew, with his profound complex of election, his need of sensuous satisfaction qualifying his every expression of personal life, and his short pendulum-swing between mystical orthodoxy and a sterile ethical culture — can he become the commentator, the arbiter, of American art and American thinking?

One of the books on my list, in the attempt to do just this, answers, without suspecting it, the question. In "Our America" Waldo Frank gives us what must be — since it is an American unguessed of the average American — the country of the intellectual affiliations of his group.

It is a country centered in New York, with a small New English ell in the rear and a rustic gazebo in Chicago; the rest of it is magnificently predicated from a car window. There is some excellent matter in the book concerning Puritanism and pioneers, which, since these are the only elements collated and partly digested by other minds, are the only elements Mr. Frank sees as contributing to our national character. There is interesting, discriminating comment on the New England writers, especially such of them as are already dead. The rest of the book is chiefly concerned with Mr. Frank's own coterie and those outside writers who have done selected work. This includes the younger Chicago group, Sandburg, Anderson, Masters, and Dreiser. Two women are mentioned as having stimulated American thought; they are Amy Lowell and Emma Goldman. There is also a footnote somewhere in the book admitting the existence of other poets and critics, and "several novelists." And in New York there are Mr. Frank's friends solemnly engaged in "releasing the soul of America," "organizing an American tradition which shall . . . bring to birth an articulated people," "quite simply . . . creating a consciousness of American life." The names of these gentlemen are Stieglitz, Stein, Ornstein, Rosenfeld, Oppenheim, Mencken, Littel, Hackett, and Brooks.

Characteristic of the New York attitude toward the vast America of our affections is a chapter on the Southwest stuffed with encyclopedic information about the Aztecs, who never occupied the territory of the United States, and some superficial observations of Pueblo Indians. It is totally void of any reference to such writers as Fewkes, Hodges, Lumholtz, Lummis, Cather, Mathews, Cushing, and Alice Fletcher. Yet the debt of American literature to Washington Mathews and Frank Cushing has no parallel in Europe, unless it be Germany's debt to the Grimm Brothers, or England's to Malory. And it is impossible to get the general relation of the work of Masters, Sandburg, and Anderson to American life without some understanding of the work of Alice Fletcher, which preceded theirs by some years.

This utter blankness to the sources of form and social inspiration is equally apparent in nearly all the comment of New York magazines devoted to the same high, self-descried mission of pointing American genius the way it should go, the same studied neglect of any indication of the way it may be going.

One of them, whose very name dedicates it to our native newness, gives 73 per cent of a year's reviewing space to non-American matter. This leaves out of account about 10 per cent of the whole space where the name of the author was unfamiliar to me and neither the review nor the publisher's announcement furnished any clue to the book's derivation. One knows, in the absence of such indices, that Thorstein Veblen is an American, and that there is no hall-mark of nationality to the sociological abstractions which he so competently handles. But why should a story by Zona Gale be so reviewed that the uninitiated reader does not know whether it happened in Wisconsin or in Senegambia — since the important contribution that Miss Gale has to make is the delimitation of life in the small American community? And is the distinction between two such poets as Louis Untermeyer and Alfred Noyes vested solely in the differences of their respective literary endowments? Is not there a great deal to be said about the distinctions which arise from one's being the product of an almost cloistral English university and the other's being the well-found, smartly schooled, urban American? Surely, if writing and the criticism of writing is to become an aid to that development of the American consciousness to which the New York critic is devoted, some relating of the work to its generating sources is indispensable. It is the absence of such feeling, grounded on ignorance of anything that the book might be related to, which gives to the New York magazine review the fructifying power of a dried specimen in a herbarium, and which accounts for the rise in importance and popularity of the newspaper Sunday Supplement review section. For newspapers are obliged to treat books as news, and news they are, if of nothing but the poverty of man's invention, and good news, whatever they contain, to the extent of their capacity to express, and so in turn to affect, our living.

To the American writer who happens not to be of the New York elect, the ascendancy of the provincial New York reviewer is a deep exasperation. Vain our search for the American form if in the end we are to be judged without any reference to the forces in American life out of which such a form should spring. And how, in hours of indecision, are we to trust to criteria which have already proved themselves to be burrs in the tail of our American Pegasus?

Take, for example, the movement toward what is styled free verse, which is loudly acclaimed by New York to have risen upon the American scene since 1912 under the patronage of Miss Lowell. As early as 1904 we were discussing it in the English Club at Stanford University and were linking it by the help of the Japanese students there with its genetic Oriental source. Many experiments were tried, and two plays that I know of in this medium actually were produced, one of them in New York as early as 1911, though it was written five years earlier. And so utterly dropped at the tail of events was New York criticism of the time that publishers insisted for the first publication of one of these plays that the lines should be written to simulate prose as a protection against urban obtuseness.

Then there was the movement represented in New York by the Provincetown Players. Practically every experiment tried by them can be found in the annals of the Little Country Theater of North Dakota. Even now there is arising in another part of the country that new metrical medium, based on intrinsic American rhythms, which William Archer long ago predicted as indispensable to the reestablishment of poetic drama. But what New York critic has heard of it?

At a recent convention of community enterprises at Washington it was made clear that the United States will no longer accept the dominance of New York in recreation, in communal ritual and celebration, in music as an element of community life, or in painting. The centralization of publishing trades in and around Manhattan alone makes it possible for New York to assume the postures of literary leadership which it has actually forfeited so far as the genuinely native product is concerned. It would seem, if decentralization is the only way to accomplish the release of the American genius, that decentralization must inevitably take place. New York criticism — we have the critic's own word for it — intends the best in the world by America. It can hardly escape their notice much longer that America begins to be possessed of a definite intention toward New York.

NOTES

1. *Earth Horizon* (1932; reprint, Albuquerque: Univ. of New Mexico Press, 1991), 330.
2. *Earth Horizon*, 352.
3. *Earth Horizon*, 349.
4. *Earth Horizon*, 354.
5. *Earth Horizon*, 354.

In spite of Austin's opinion that New York editors took "too narrow a sweep" in their perspective, the same persistence that got her into editorial offices sometimes got her into print as well. During 1920, Austin wrote a series of essays for the Nation *about one of her more far-reaching interests, U.S. relations with Mexico. "Wanted: A New Method in Mexico" appeared on 21 February.*

Austin's thinking about Mexico had been developing for some time, an outgrowth of her interest in folk movements and the Native American and Hispanic heritages of the Southwest. Like others on the Greenwich Village scene, she had watched closely the developments of the Mexican Revolution that began in earnest with the ouster of Porfirio Diaz in 1911. In 1920, Mexico was well into its own "new method." Venustiano Carranza seemed for the time almost firmly in power. Zapata had been killed in 1919, and the other rival revolutionary factions were quiet. The constitution of 1917 had been in place almost three years, placing important limits on the activities of the American "interests" Austin warns against here. Even if Austin does not employ the more impassioned tone taken by her New York acquaintances John Reed or Max Eastman writing in the Masses *about the revolution, she does draw upon the general current of Greenwich Village socialism in her commentary. Austin stresses the uniqueness of the Mexican culture and heritage, noting that its "ten-thousand-year-old inheritance of communistic living" does not easily adapt to the imposed economic models of the United States. She speaks for tolerance, difference, and restraint. "We have been led to conclude," she writes, "rather amiably but mistakenly, that what all struggling nations want is exactly what we have got for ourselves." Using Mexico as a close, specific instance, she elaborates with an understated practical argument the case against the cultural bias and economic imperialism that many liberals and self-styled radicals like Austin had seen characterizing U.S. foreign relations since the Spanish-American War.*

Wanted: A New Method in Mexico

It is obvious that the United States is approaching a point in its relations to Mexico that has many items in common with our approach to the Great War. The moment at which we could have taken a deciding tone toward Mexico on the high ground of an affirmative international policy having been allowed to slip past, we have become bitterly involved with our sister republic over a sordid question of oil wells, and under the pressure of European interests. In spite of the Monroe Doctrine we are in such a position in regard to Mexico that unless a new method is evolved, within six or eight months we may not only find ourselves embroiled on our own account, but we may have four or five South American countries and at least two European countries against us.

It is true we have shambled into this pocket foremost position largely because of the propaganda of what are known as "the interests." Certain small groups who have money invested in Mexico, or see it as a field for future investment, have found their business interfered with by what has been going on there lately. That is to say, they have found that they cannot do business by the same methods that they employ in doing business with us. The result is an active propaganda, financed by those interests, to have the United States forcibly remake the economic system of Mexico as nearly as possible like the one under which "the interests" have thriven so well in England and America.

It is perfectly safe to say that three-fifths of our present difficulty with Mexico is of this hand-made variety. The banditry of which so much is made in the newspapers is in no sense a part of our effort at internationalism. As much of it as is not due to the same sorts of conditions that are producing disorder in the rest of the world, is due to the struggle of outside capitalists among themselves. Capitalists in the United Sates and elsewhere have sold arms to Mexicans, smuggling them in in defiance of the Mexican Government for the purpose of preventing other

Reprinted from *The Nation* magazine, 110 (1920). © The Nation Company, Inc.

capitalists from making more profit out of Mexican mines and oil fields. All this is a matter of common knowledge and has been a steadily shaping force in determining the attitude which the Latin-American republics are beginning to take toward us.

But no such attempt against the integrity of the United States and the rights and dignities of Mexico could become a factor if it were not for characteristic weaknesses of the American people, the same weaknesses which have brought us into equally undesirable and contradictory relations with Russia. Chief of these weaknesses is our total lack of the historic sense, the failure to recognize and measure the element of social continuity. Through this lack of acquaintance with the source and direction of history, we have been led to conclude, rather amiably but mistakenly, that what all struggling nations want is exactly what we have got for ourselves. We begin by thinking about the people of Mexico as Mexicans, or at the best as Spanish and Indian, not at all as Aztecs, Yucatecs, and Yaquis, or other allied but by no means affiliated, and only partially federated, peoples. We think of the struggles going on there as solely political, the struggle between petty political chiefs. We have not at all considered whether the disposition of the Mexican groups to arise and slay one another occasionally may not have a touch of that "inevitable" which we concede to the disharmonies of our own blacks and whites. We have not sufficiently realized that there are many battles between the opposing forces in Mexico which result in fewer casualties than one of our own race riots. We have not even, through our recent tough with the hereditary antagonisms of southeastern Europe, taken the measure of such facts as that Yucatan was never really a part of Mexico any more than Ukrainia was a part of Russia, that Yaqui Land was never really conquered even by the Spanish, and that to these long-standing difficulties we are adding a lively Balkan hate along our Texan border.

These alien and warring states were forcibly federated by Spain and are now striving to refederate themselves in view of their common economic destiny, on a basis of common agreement. Such a refederation would seem to be important to the peace of the western world. But before the United States attempts to assist at the process without an invitation, it would be well to consider whether we could actually accomplish any more than Spain did for the integration of the Mexican peoples.

The ideal of an experienced and powerful nation maintaining order while the process of interpenetration of group consciousness is going on between dissimilar peoples with a common objective, is one to be treated seriously. But just how far, when history is one of the protagonists, can the United States travel on an unpracticed, well-meaning idealism? Recent events in Europe would suggest that we have not gone far. Certainly we have not got beyond the stage of barbarous slaughter between our own unassimilated — and by all our policies rated as inassimilable — races. And if the history of Bohemia and Poland and Czechoslovakia left us in any doubt as to whether integration can be accomplished by forcibly squashing together dissimilar national elements, there is India. There it has been tried under the nearest approach to American methods, but the only group consciousness which shows itself is the common consciousness of England as an oppressor; and the only unification evident is that of the desire to throw off the English rule.

When the American people involved themselves in Russia in a situation which belies their real faith in the democratic principle, it was because of an almost universal conviction that what the Russian people wanted was another United States.

There is an equally mistaken and probably sincere idea abroad about Mexico, an idea that the majority of the Mexican people really want political and industrial conditions like ours and won't be happy until we go in and cram them down their throats. In spite of our mistake about Russia, now slowly yielding to contradicting facts, we not only go on making this mistake about Mexico, but we are basing all our arguments in favor of force on this same racial inability of the Mexican to adapt himself to our economic system. This system, which in general goes by the title of capitalism, has been in our history and our blood since the Roman Empire. It was never in the history or in the blood of Mexico. Not only has it had no part in their natural economic evolution, but their nearest approach to a system like ours during the past two hundred years, carries with it associations of cruelty and oppression for which we have no measure. Possibly, if left to herself for the centuries Spain oppressed her, Mexico might have moved toward capitalism, as so many other nations have entered by that gate. But at present, except for a brief forced period, about two thousand years of economic evolution lie between Mexican economic adjustments and ours. Even the banditry so disturbing to their peace and ours is an instance of their native disposition toward group activity; the lone "bad man" is no more found among them than the solitary captain of industry.

Let me illustrate one of those differences of economic approach, which our failure to estimate the force of historic continuity prevents the average American citizen from realizing. Everybody understands that land hunger is a contributive element in the revolutions of both Russia and Mexico. Everybody wanted land and wanted it so acutely that in the early days of both revolutions, as soon as a piece of land had been allotted to them, numbers of the revolutionists sat down upon it with the revolution half finished. But here in the United States we missed the significance of the fact that the particular kind of land most mentioned in this connection in Mexico was the *ejido*. It was the dispossession of the towns of their *ejidos* which was reckoned to have set the revolution in train. The restoration of the *ejidos* was one of Carranza's earliest projects, and it was to effect this that confiscations of property were made. The *ejido* was the land *owned in common by the community*, and its significance for us lies in the light it throws on land ownership in general in Mexico.

With us land is property. Farming is a "business." With the Mexican, land was environment. It was domain. Holding land by title is a recent Spanish innovation, the native Mexican never having thought of such a thing as private property in land. That this form persists to some extent, a "hang-over" from the Spanish invasion, does not alter the essentials of the agrarian problem in Mexico. Historically and racially it is a problem in *relationship* rather than in possession.

The people of Yucatan and some parts of the south come nearer being farmers in our sense of the word, since their preoccupation is chiefly with the product of the soil. But in Mexico proper, people do not so much live off of the land as live on it. By racial genius they are craftsmen of a superior sort, and their crafts, building, metal working, weaving, and ceramics, draw their inspiration from being related in groups to the land and the resources of the land.

Social psychologists and even the newspapers are beginning to talk about group psychology as the developing factor in politics, just as group action is rapidly becoming the determining factor in economics. But group psychology and group action are the native Mexican's atmosphere, they are all his past. They are deep enough to give to the present movement of Mexican nationalism its direction toward a communism of land and natural resources older and more instinctive than anything of the kind that we have to deal with in Russia. This instinct is not so articulate as it is in Russia. The Mexicans have not thought so much nor so informedly about their situation. Masses of them have not thought at all; they have simply moved by the impetus of their own history in the inevitable direction. Far from being obsessed by a desire to overthrow the capitalistic system, millions of them are at a loss to understand why their own instinctive readjustment, following the dislocation of the past three hundred years, should be looked upon with hostility by our system. So they naturally read self-interest into any motion of ours toward interfering with the processes of that readjustment.

Public opinion has made very much the same mistake about the present political leaders in Mexico that it has made in Russia. It has persisted in seeing them as a little group of radicals instead of a racially representative group of Mexicans, and their ideas as remote from the Mexican masses, on no better ground than that they are unfamiliar to us. There is even a general idea that if we could only see some other group in power, besides the Carranzistas, we should see a very different economic disposition. But no turn of the political wheel is ever going to put anybody but Mexicans into power in Mexico. It might put base and corruptible groups into power, but they would still be made up from the three classes of the Mexican people: Creoles, of pure Spanish descent born for several generations in Mexico, and full inheritors of a native Spanish aptitude for politics; or Mestizos and Indians with their ten-thousand-year-old inheritance of communistic living, and particularly of communism in land and natural resources. And when we see the present leaders in Mexico as the conscious element of the masses moving instinctively in line with their own history, we must see them as succeeding so well that if we really mean to interfere with the process, they have put us in the worst possible position for doing so.

But is there any real advantage in our attempting to pick up a nation of sixteen million people and jump them over two thousand years of economic development in two or three? Europe, and especially England, would profit by our attempt. But who in America, with the exception of a few of our capitalists, would profit by having a neighbor in a state of economic catalepsy, batted about by "the interests" at our expense? What we really want is an amicable relation with a country in a normal state of productiveness, capable of equable economic exchange. Let our statesmen accept the intimations of history and racial genius. Let them realize that Mexico cannot be made over on the American economic plan. Let them once for all give up this abortive attempt, and address themselves not to forcing an alien method on the Mexican people, but to finding a method by which two dissimilar economic systems can live together amicably.

Within the next generation this has got to be done. Nobody can be such a fool as to imagine that all the nations of Europe are to emerge from their present confusion with the old-style economic arrangements. Some countries are going to come back to do business at the old stand, temporarily, at least, on a new and more communistic basis. It may not be Russia; it may be Germany; and if we do not interfere it certainly will be Mexico. And the other countries will have to learn to do business under these new conditions. Why not America first?

The American way of doing business is the expression of the American temperament in relation to its environment. In the past it has been characterized by a large adaptability. As a republic, we learned to do business very successfully with monarchies, and we should also be able to do business with Mexico even under the modern conditions of nationalized natural resources, unless American business has already reached that fussy condition of middle age in which it can do business only in its own way; and if that is the case, it will meet the inevitable defeat of middle age in attempting to prescribe the procedure of developing nationalities.

After recovering from a severe illness and while alternating work on The Land of Journeys' Ending *and* The American Rhythm, *Austin took time off to visit England in 1922. "I had no trouble finding the Fabians," she writes, "except that Joseph Conrad, with whom I renewed acquaintance, kept telling me that the Fabians were no longer the intellectual leaders, and that I was wasting my time on them."[1] In spite of Conrad's warning, the urbane evolutionary socialism of the Fabian society, as well as the personal presence of its founders and luminaries — George Bernard Shaw and Beatrice and Sidney Webb — remained a strong attraction. Austin lectured at the society's 1922 summer school, trying out in public presentation many of the developing arguments about the environmental inherency of poetic form that would take more complete shape the next year in* The American Rhythm.

Austin's attendance among the Fabians reflects her lifelong gravitation toward literary circles, if not formal movements. Inviting Sinclair Lewis to come along for tea with Shaw and company, Austin remarks that "there was an air about them of being liked, of belonging, like the feeling we had once for the group at Carmel."[2] But beyond this sense of intellectual fellow-feeling, Austin's interest in Fabianism signals a point of connection between the aesthetic theories she was then exploring in her work on The American Rhythm *and the argument she persistently advanced concerning the value of the native "socialism" she observed, or posited, among indigenous Americans. Similarly, her sharp reaction while in Stow-on-Wold to May Sinclair's opposition to "the idea that novels should be written about social problems"[3] suggests the militancy underlying Austin's writing during her residency in New York and the appeal of the agenda of education and social change pursued by the Fabians.*

It was in how to interpret and apply this shared perspective in an American context that Austin parted with her hosts. Of Beatrice and Sidney Webb, she remarks: "They had the weakness that most English people have in talking with Americans, that of assuming to know everything there is to know about America, and that anything that is not English is negligible."[4] When asked why women's magazines would not flourish in London the way they did in America, Austin concluded that "in London people were half women and half ladies, but in the United States they were, whether ladies or not, always women."[5] The same issue of the Bookman *in which appears "My Fabian Summer" also contains "The Poems of the Month," selected by Carl Sandburg, including Austin's "Woman's Song," originally published in* Harper's.

from My Fabian Summer

During the first decade of the present century the most coveted and hazardous adventure of the English-speaking Intellectual, was being invited to address the Fabian Society. It met weekly at King's Hall, presided over by a fox-colored half-god, with a barely perceptible brogue and a habit of kicking up the cloven hoofs of his mind in a manner so engaging that you forgave him for having at the same time kicked the dust of obliquity on yours. There were, of course speakers who declined to meet Mr. Shaw in debate on the ground that he kicked dust in proportion as he found himself unable to meet your thrust. What I suspect is that nobody knew whether G. B. S. could meet an argument or not, since by the time the argument had reached its destination, he had already moved on to his next position.

The Fabians are Socialists, but to the American whose associations with the word are all of Rand School and red neckties, it must be explained that the relation of Fabian Socialism to Marxian, is about the relation of early Christianity to Methodism. Fabianism in its best days was an incandescent state of mind in the heat of which the existing social order was expected to drop noiselessly into ash. Permeation rather than political action was its method, and the history of its interests provides the stuffing for a full-sized book. Besides Shaw it numbered H. G. Wells, and Sidney and Beatrice Webb, to mention only easily recognizable names among its members. Whoever survived a Fabian debate with enough of his original intellectual integument to cover his quivering soul, could thereafter count himself among the intellectually considerable.

About the end of the decade, Mr. Wells, whose mind began to itch for the world horizons that have since engaged his attention, thought it time for the Society to emerge from its perpetual discussion into a competent political instrument. The Webbs thought not, with the result that it was finally Wells who emerged

Originally published in the *Bookman* 54 (1921). Reprinted by permission of the School of American Research.

— spent missiles of the encounter strew the field of radical literature of that time — leaving the Fabians securely "Webbed," as he put it, in the factual entanglement of the Minority Poor Law Report. There were other defections and offshoots, notably the Guild Socialists, but it was to the parent society that I found myself engaged this summer in the character of American Lecturer, not without misgivings that the Fabians couldn't be what they once were, or they wouldn't have had me. Could I have imagined that the implications of a Fabian summer included fox trotting with George Bernard Shaw and acting a leading part in my own play burlesquing one of our most valued institutions to which I myself had played prophet, I should probably have avoided it, and so lost the most memorable of my European vacations.

The Fabian Summer School for this year occupied the premises of a large private school at Prior's Field in the lovely shire of Surrey, during the month of August. There was a sprinkling of Americans in attendance, and a professional Irishman come down from London to explain that the Irish Revolutionists were more long-suffering and noble-souled than any other revolutionists (which is very likely the case). This information did not, however, in the least affect the characteristic British detachment of the Fabians. That was what struck the Americans, the preponderance of local English interests, and the fact that whether it were the League of Nations, Irish Freedom, or the Rates that was discussed, there was an apparent failure to evoke the disposition to do something about it which characterizes American gatherings of this quality. If it had not been for an experience which I shall undertake later and probably unsuccessfully to describe, I might have been still in the dark as to how the "permeation" of the English mind by the Fabian doctrine is accomplished. . . .

To most people outside of England, the Webbs, Sidney and Beatrice, and Bernard Shaw *are* the Fabians. As an example of the imposing, the monumental impression that can be made by a married pair working in entire intellectual complement, the Webbs are unsurpassed. It is to them the Fabians owe the sky-piled pyre of economic fact on which it is expected the existing social order will finally be immolated. I seldom feel that conflagration so near at hand as I did when I heard Beatrice Webb tell the assembled Fabians that prayer is one of the indispensable items of successful economic and sociological research. We worked over that ground pretty thoroughly the next morning, Mrs. Webb and the American Lecturer, pacing up and down the grass walk, touching the necessity of saturating all our experiences of the heart or of the intellect in the older, more experienced layers of being, before suffering them to crystallize as forms of social procedure.

It was directly afterward that I had the experience before referred to, of admission to the collective mind of the English.

It was the quiet end of the afternoon; there was a hot smell of roses in the air, pricked from every corner of the lovely English gardens with shafts of cheerful laughter. I was leaning against the parapet by the lily pond, thinking of nothing in particular when, by such degrees that I am unable to fix the precise moment of its happening, England laid a warm, covering hand on me. What had been an American observer was lost in the sudden onset and lapsing of wave on wave of intimacy so perfect that it was only by the narrowest margin of alien consciousness that I was aware of what was going on in me. No, it was not because, like most people, I have inherited English strains. I'm French too, yet permanently outside the French consciousness. I'm Scotch also, by descent, but besides thinking that a handsome Scot is the handsomest of men, I have no Celtic affinities. It was simply that the collective English mind had widened suddenly and made room for me. This is the peculiar gift of the English, the source of their genius for politics which has distinguished them among nations.

Perhaps this inclusion in the English consciousness, which was not for this occasion only, had something to do with my falling so readily into the Shavian cult when Mr. Shaw came down for the whole of the last week; for how could Shaw so successfully alternately tickle and annoy the public sense of England if we were not completely inside it? One recognizes him instantly, quite the tallest man in any company, straight as a pine that has stayed a full-orbed moon on its top. The fox-colored hair and beard have gone moon-white around the Indian summer glow of his face, reflecting the autumnal mellowness of his mind.

There is an extraordinarily clean-blown look about Shaw at sixty-five, such a windy, star-bright look as one surprises occasionally at the edge of October evenings. Of the Irish impishness that made him once so exasperating in debate, there is left spiritual dexterity that pricks you to join him in what must never be mistaken as a statement of Shaw's belief, but the search for that which is worthy to be believed.

It is this search for reality informing all his talk, that makes Shaw so misleading to quote. He suffers the fate of all brilliant people, that of being lost in the blaze in his own fireworks. What he said to the Fabians was the speech of a Socialist to Socialists, and not to be attempted by the uninitiate. Of things said in conversation, besides the impression of an incorruptible geniality, there remain glints and flashes. . . . "Irish independence? Well, I'm a Socialist, I'm not so much for independence, . . . interdependence . . . a characteristic island civilization. We might produce it . . . we've never really had an island parliament, you know. . . . "

"Birth control . . . what right have you to say to life, It shall not be? How do you know you didn't struggle with your parents to be born as much as ever parents struggled to prevent you . . . a continuing process of life. . . . What do we really *know*!"

"What's a book, once it's done?" he said. "My books mean very little to me . . . the finish to a phase of thinking. . . . Tell your niece not to go into the theatre unless she can't help it. As a career it's not worth it . . . it's an expression . . . one must be satisfied to be used."

Finally we talked of his coming to America. That was at Hern Bay, where the Guild Socialists were in session. At Canterbury seven miles away I had run into Sinclair Lewis coming out of the Cathedral Close, and learned that he had sold 300,000 copies of his book. What else could I do but produce my own particular counter-irritant, that I was on terms with G. B. S. which permitted me to take promising young American authors to tea with him without waiting to be invited. Mr. Shaw does not really take tea, which gave him more time to talk. This he did, looking not unlike some ancient pagan deity consenting to be pleased with mortals. Meanwhile we held our cups and breathed softly not to break the spell. W. K. Ratcliffe was there, and one or two Guilders. I recall a lad with a stiff leg and a distinguished service order and the engrossed, uplifted watchfulness of a happy dog, eyes on his master. . . . I asked G. B. if it were true that he had refused a million dollars for his film rights because the producer had insisted on talking art when Shaw wished to talk money.

It was true, he admitted, twinkling reminiscently over the kind of art talk an American film manager had been primed with, expressly to talk to Shaw. "But the truth was," said G. B., "That I had my lawyer figure it out for me, and found that after I had paid the American tax, the English tax, and the super-taxes on that million, I should be about fifteen thousand dollars out of pocket."

We wished to know if that meant that he would never come to the United States at all. The only other way that the possibility had been presented to him, had been to be led about by a lecture bureau and exhibited for the most money. "How could I let a man sign up for me, when I might say something the first day that would upset all his calculations?" he protested.

What I proposed was that we should form a Shaw Committee which would permit him the greatest number of public appearances compatible with entire personal freedom. "I ought to have come ten years ago," he said. But at the last there was yielding in his look. It could be managed I think. It should be managed. Even if the only way is to invite the Fabian Society to hold its next summer session in New York.

NOTES

1. *Earth Horizon* (1932; reprint, Albuquerque: Univ. of New Mexico Press, 1991), 342.
2. *Earth Horizon*, 342.
3. *Earth Horizon*, 341.
4. *Earth Horizon*, 342.
5. *Earth Horizon*, 344.

Four years after she charted a course for women to pursue their newly gained political franchise in The Young Woman Citizen, *Austin extended her project to the task of improving the analytical and critical skills of women as interpreters of public events and cultural activity. In the essay "Women as Audience," Austin points out the subordination of women in American "androcentric culture" to the role of "passive spectator to the male performance." For Austin, women's complicity in the authority of the patriarchal voice in all areas of public life is both what is most galling and most readily susceptible to change.*

Austin focuses her criticism on the then burgeoning women's club movement, which in the name of cultural enrichment sponsored organized book readings and provided an extensive public lecture forum. Although women's clubs accounted for many of Austin's own lecture fees during the 1920s, she attacks them for their failure to teach women how "to enter into the creative struggle." Austin's notion of audience implies active, critical reception. The ineffectiveness of the clubs in promoting independent critical thought among their some four million members represented for Austin the need to recognize the central role literature and other forms of creative practice play in shaping social change, as well as the need for women to take control of their own responses as creative acts in themselves. The same Bookman *issue contains work by Sandburg, Dreiser, and Atherton. John Farrar's "Literary Spotlight" feature focuses on F. Scott Fitzgerald.*

Women as Audience

Among the most resented attitudes to which women have been reduced by our androcentric culture, is that of passive spectator to the male performance. The whole feminist movement, in fact, is energized by our resistance to that role, and our determination to participate in constructive movement by contact. It is disconcerting then, to discover, after the removal of the political bar, that in everything but the personal accomplishment we are still in a state of practical nullity toward our national culture, owing to our never having learned, as women, the business of being audience. All that we have learned, it now appears, is the art of sitting still in more or less becoming attitudes.

It is a humiliating admission for so confirmed a feminist as myself to make, but a survey of what is actually transacting among the organized and federated groups of women from whom creative social reaction might have been expected, shows them, in respect to literature, art, and education, very much in the state of those conscientious attendants at concerts who have to wait until the conductor turns around to know when to applaud the orchestra. Any public performer who is clever enough to make the applausive gesture at suitable intervals can be sure of a sufficient feminine claque to keep him circulating in the Big Time of platform attention without any particular deserts.

Consider in this connection, the fate of recent European candidates for the American claque as they have enfilladed across our lecture field. Whenever they have been of sufficient prominence to attract mixed audiences of men and women, those who had nothing to say found themselves swiftly and emphatically curtailed in their opportunities of saying it. Few laurels of alien growth have ever been sprouted vigorously enough in the atmosphere of self-conscious democracy, to conceal the want of pertinence in the wearer of them. But when the lecturer is of the type whose access to the American pocketbook is chiefly by way of

Originally published in the *Bookman* 55 (1922). Reprinted by permission of the School of American Research.

the stereotyped women's organizations, the shadow of a leaf upon his brow — less, the mere poise of that brow as if it wore the wreath — is enough to insure his thrift campaign against frost. After a few months of circulation among women's club audiences he will be in a position to command the top price from the New York magazines for telling the American public the low opinion he has formed of its native culture.

Not that I would deny to, say, W. L. George, such confirmation of his estimate of the inferior intelligence of women as he derives from those who can be brought together to hear him express it. What I am here to affirm is that neither the ease with which American women can be intellectually imposed upon, nor their failure to function creatively as audience to our burgeoning literature and art, is to be taken as indicative of any lack of capacity critically to appreciate, or individually to produce their share of it. It has to do with the general inexperience of women in collective reaction, and is about as indicative as the movements of a waltzing horse of what could normally be expected.

Let me illustrate from the women's magazines, which are theoretically created in response to what the editors, assisted by the advertisers, really know of what women want. Actually, in addition to their function as trade journals, which they admirably fill, women's magazines represent what the men editors think it desirable for women to read, modified by the erroneous conviction of advertisers that the spread of advanced ideas among women lessens the consumption of bottled mincemeat, colored insert breakfast food, and full-page flour. There was "The Ladies' Home Journal" which, under Mr. Bok, built up an unprecedented standard of magazine popularity. At the same time it failed to retard in the slightest degree the successful development of all the ideas it opposed — suffrage, women's clubs, family limitation and the like — which went on progressively among the very women on whose living room tables the "Journal" was periodically displayed.

It is this curious lack of causality between what women unprotestingly take in, and what they can be counted on to do, that inhibits the free expression of woman-mindedness in our literature and art. There is no more sequential relation between what they listen to and what they think, than there is between their morals and the things they can be induced to sit through in the moving picture houses.

The photodrama provides us with one of the most illuminating side lights on the failure of women to function representatively as audience, in their neglect of the quality of "form" in cultural expression. The criterions of women are interior. What was meant, what was subjectively felt by the protagonists, determines for them the effectuality of the action. High ground for this interior standard being established by convention, an audience of women can not only be made to accept, but can be induced to applaud offenses against essential decency. Let it be clearly understood that the boudoir scene is an incident in a proper honeymoon, and details which every man in the audience knows were introduced with libidinous intent, will "get by" with the women. On the same general level this is true of books. In the second rank of popular magazines, one feels certain, we are saved from a great deal of potential indecency only by the circumstances of their being read largely by men.

I have lectured many times before women audiences, on the social significance of literature, and I have made a habit of setting down immediately afterward the significant questions asked, with the result that, turning them over just now, I find not one indicative of the desire, or the sense of obligation on the part of the reader, to enter into the creative struggle. What they do seem to want is suggestions for obtaining creative *results* for themselves, or items by which they may participate effectively in the *talk* about created work. Or they will be satisfied with mere entertainment.

Much of this detachment is, I suspect, the residue of woman's century old habit of thinking of books, magazines, plays, and painting as the sort of thing Daddy brings home from his hunting, toward which she has conceived her duty to be an uncritical disposition to make the best of what is offered. Thus there is always a tendency on the part of women to measure art by the ensuing fatness of their personal reactions, rather than by the social significance of the creative act; to be appreciative of the artist as a man rather than as a representative of the tribe of mankind. It may be that the slight touch of the exotic attaching to the foreign poet and novelist, which favors this feminine attitude of superior detachment from the sweat of achieving, has something to do with their preferential hearing. For the rest we have no evidence that Xanthippe thought any more highly of the "Dialogues" than Carol Kennicott thought of the symposium at the drug store.

If it were not for the circumstances that few women's clubs can be induced to pay to women artists the terms and attention that are conceded to men, the track to effective participation might be beaten out for them by women who have already trodden it for themselves. No doubt much of the collective ineffectiveness of women in this field is due to their never having acquired free movement of themselves as impersonal, unemphasized items of society.

An incident of constant recurrence in the life of every woman who has attained a reasonable literary expression of herself, is to be importuned by other women to write about this, to protest against that, or to write more often on matters concerning which it is her consuming desire to be permitted to write. When she responds with an impatient, "For heaven's sake, if you like my stuff, don't waste time telling me, tell the editor!" the most usual retort is a startled, "But he wouldn't pay any attention to me, I'm no critic." This is something more than an excessive estimate of the part critics play in the establishment of literary reputations. It is both evidence and result of woman's inexperience in functioning as a particle of the democratic whole. Accustomed immemorially to presenting herself as an individual issue, as maiden, wife, mother, at the lowest as female, she tends still to approach the cultural poll in some specialized capacity. It is news to her that as paying member of the audience she has acquired both privilege and obligation in respect to the quality of the performance. Some day it will come to her, together with the horrid thought that she has been excluded this long time from cultural effectiveness, not by man's wish to exclude her, but because she has never learned the game.

It must be failure of method. Nobody could accuse the women's clubs of any failure of intention to do their whole duty by the literature of their native land. Have they not every one of them a book committee, and the habit of inviting visiting celebrities to sit on the platform whole afternoons at the price of saying a few words at the end of the regular program? Has not every author in America had one or more letters stating that the writer's club has assigned that particular author to her for author's day, and she has never read any of his works; will he not kindly send her a review of his life and works to read? Do not thousands of dollars pass annually by way of their lecture committees to the pockets of authors of whom nobody can say with certainty where, in the scheme of American values, they belong?

It would be unfair to attribute the failure of one of the most remarkable organizations ever created in any society, to produce an appreciable effect on our literature, to the four million women of the finer strain who make up its membership. Is not the whole situation a reflection of our common national disposition to regard all art as a performance, some kind of "show"? Whereas the artist himself knows it is a way of life, of which the book or the picture is the evidence rather than the object of pursuit. It is not likely that men, just as men, would do any better. But because women have rather definitely assumed the role of patrons of culture, because they have made a stagger at fulfilling it, they must come in for a certain amount of question. It is women who have already accepted the responsibility for social conditions in which mature men and women divide themselves, for the purposes of culture, according to sex. So when we wish to talk about organized effort to produce a representative culture, we have nothing else to talk about but the women's clubs. European observers are disposed to credit this state of things to a want of sex power in our women; that is, to a feebleness in the whole delicate complex of vital responses which women make to men. It is interesting to note that Sinclair Lewis, whether deliberately or by one of those divine accidents to which the sincere artist is liable, related these two impotencies in the heroine of "Main Street." But such an explanation proceeds primarily from the old view that men produce and women appreciate; a state of things which our whole American experiment is organized to deny. The most we can say of

American women is that they have rejected the traditional mode of response to intellectual creativeness, without having taught themselves any more efficacious measures.

What women have to learn to be audience to, is not the book after it is written, nor the personality of the author who writes it, but the process by which a really vital book gets itself produced out of our communal experience. What they must assist at is not the adumbration of praise for work that is done, so much as the selection and emphasis of social conditions that have power over a book while it is doing. In this connection an Author's League as much interested in what of the author is going into the book, as in what is coming back to him in the way of royalties, might be helpful.

It is a realization of the need of women to rehearse the role of audience in the collective key, that has led to the organization of the Women's News Service, by which, through the medium of their local press, women will be enabled to practice, along lines already familiar, the rapid intake and response indispensable to their success as coefficients of a democratic culture. But the Women's News Service aims only at establishing this rapport about what women are doing. What is needed is a realization that in the indigenous literature of America, there already exists a competent news service about life as it is living. The true approach to it from women is neither as women nor as critics, but as participators in the collective experience, of which the particular mode of poetry or fiction is the individual expression. Such an approach is neither instinctive in women, nor part of their social inheritance. It cannot, however, be assumed that men sitting together as an organized body to hear any available author read from or talk about his work, will produce any sort of result which will be found competent to support a creditable national literature. Critical response must be learned, and to be of constructive value in the great age of American literature, must begin to be operative shortly. Otherwise it might be suspected that the role to which men assigned women, of sitting still and saying nothing except what is pleasant, is the one to which they are intrinsically best adapted.

"The American Form of the Novel" appeared in a special issue of the New Republic titled "The Novel of Tomorrow and the Scope of Fiction," along with Willa Cather's "The Novel Demeuble" and Theodore Dreiser's "The Scope of Fiction," as well as essays by Samuel Hopkins Adams, Zona Gale, James Branch Cabell, Floyd Dell, and Waldo Frank. Dreiser, for one, imagined the realist fiction that would result "if we could throw all the furniture out of the window."[1]

Although she is generally regarded as outside the main current of literary modernism (an eddy familiar to writers who have become associated with regional settings and concerns), in this essay, published in the same year that Joyce's Ulysses established new paradigms for both content and form in twentieth-century fiction, Austin makes a structural analysis of literature fundamentally modernist in its impulse. She anticipates her later arguments (most prominently made in The American Rhythm, 1923) for literary structure based on the experience of the natural environment and provides an early reference to her notion of an evolving, democratic "collective consciousness" in American society based on changing gender roles and on a phenomenological awareness of experienced place.

If modern American life is fundamentally "inchoate" and narrative form hence unreliable, Austin feels justified in exploring the possible future of the American novel in later turning to what she sees as the genuine originality of Native American verse forms for a model. She describes her experience hearing recordings of native song or verse and the way she understood that song or verse to suggest an environmentally determined or mediated structure: "It was when I discovered that I could listen to aboriginal verses on the phonograph in unidentified Amerindian languages, and securely refer them by their dominant rhythms to the plains, the deserts and woodlands that had produced them, that I awoke to the relationships that must necessarily exist between aboriginal and later American forms."[2]

Whether or not we accept the reliability of Austin's "secure" reference, her impulse to discover, perhaps rediscover, or maybe even invent situationally appropriate and variable narrative structure suggests her insight that fiction is just as much a matter of the arrangement of the furniture as it is the selection of the divan.

The American Form of the Novel

The novel has always concerned itself with such incidents of the life performance as have been found significant by the age in which they occur. Its scope has been combat when combat was the major occupation of men. When complete stratification had taken place in European society, the story-telling emphasis shifted to the set of circumstances by which the hero was introduced into the social strata in which he was henceforth to function. Thus, where the Greek long story was content to deal with the adventure of arms, the mediaeval romance made a feat of arms the means, subordinate to the event, of the hero's admission into high society, slaying the enemy as a prelude to marrying the king's daughter and sharing the kingdom.

When, however, the goal of man's serious endeavor became, as it did in the last century, some sort of successful escape from social certitude, the scope of the novel was extended to include the whole ground of his struggle and its various objectives. Then came America and brought a stage of things in which uncertainty multiplied as to what the objective of man's secret and incessant search should be. Except in a limited, personal sense we have never known in the United States just which of us is villain and which hero. In addition to the decay of recognized social categories, our novelists find themselves under the necessity of working out their story patterns on a set of shifting backgrounds no two of which are entirely conformable. I myself, and I suspect my experience to be typical, have had to learn three backgrounds, as distinct, except for the language spoken, as Paris, Gopher Prairie and the Scottish Highlands. While I do not complain to the gods of these things, I maintain that it gives me a disadvantage compared to Mr. Galsworthy, say, who, however rotten he finds the warp of English society to be, still finds it regularly spaced and competent to sustain the design of any story he may elect to weave.

Originally published in the *New Republic* 30 (1922). Reprinted by permission of the School of American Research.

There can be, of course, as many arrangements of the terms of individual experience as there are ways in which experience can widely happen. But these are not so many as might be supposed. Varieties of personal adventure are more or less pulled together by the social frame in which they occur. One of the recognized criterions of veracity in a novel is the question, could, or couldn't, the main incident have occurred in that fashion in a given type of society. But such a question can only be asked by people who have acquired the capacity to feel truth in respect to their own environment. It can never be asked by people for whom appreciations of pattern, as it affects the literary expression of experience, have been stereotyped to the warp of relations which are no longer admitted as social determinants. For every novel that the reviewer elects for critical attention, he discards a dozen others of possibly equal workmanship, for no reason but that they deal with patterns that have ceased to have — or perhaps never did have — constructive relation to the society in which we live. Or, in cases where high veracity and perfection of form compel his admiration, as in The Age of Innocence, he makes his point out of the very failure of validity in the background, itself a fragment of an earlier, outworn social fabric. Below the limit of a possible claim on his attention, every reviewer is also aware of scores of novels, eyeless and amorphic, kept moving on the submerged social levels by the thousands of readers who never come any nearer the surface of the present than perhaps to be occasionally chilled by it.

Aside from questions of form, is not the difference between novels which compel our attention and those we lightly discard, just this validity of relation between social warp and individual pattern? It is not necessary that the supporting structure of society appear as subject matter, but a certain clear sense of it in the writer's mind.

It is hardly possible yet in America to produce so smooth an over-woven piece as Mr. Waddington of Wyck, with the technique of one of those detached motifs of Chinese embroidery, in which, though everywhere to be traced, not one thread of the sustaining fabric is visible. Miss Sinclair works under the conviction that the social structure ought never to be treated by the novelist as part of his undertaking, but that, I suspect, is due to her never having worked on the disconcertingly spaced and frequently sleazy background of American society. What we have to look for here is the ability, on the part of the writer, to fix upon the prophetic trend of happenings. Such a novel as Main Street should sustain itself a long time as a record of our discovery of the Community as villain, or, if you feel as some of us do toward its leading lady, as hero.

It is this necessity, forced upon us by recent social developments, of finding new, because as yet undeclared, points of balance in the arrangements of the American elements of story design, that has given rise to the notion that in America the novel need not concern itself with form primarily. But this can hardly be the case if we are to think of novel writing as an art, subject to the condition of survival in time.

The novel, more than any other written thing, is an attempt to persuade, at its best to compel, men to give over for a moment the pursuit of the distant goal, and savor the color, the intensity and solidarity of experience *while it is passing.* It is of no particular moment which one of the currents of experience that loop and whirl and cascade and backwater through the stream of human existence, is selected. It is important however, that it be presented in the idiom, that is to say in the life pattern, of the audience for whom it is intended. What I mean by pattern is the arrangement of story elements in true relation to the social structure by which they are displayed. In this sense form becomes a matter of the span of perceptive consciousness of the selected audience.

This gives, in our inchoate American life, the greatest latitude of incident, but confines the novelist rather strictly to a democratic structure. It deprives him of fixed goals of social or financial or political achievement as terminal points, since none of these things have any permanence in the American scheme of things. The utmost the American novelist can hope for if he hopes at all to see his work included in the literature of his time, is that it may eventually be found to lie along in the direction of the growing tip of collective consciousness.

Preeminently the novelist's gift is that of access to the collective mind. But there is a curious secret relation between the novelist's point of access and his grasp of form — and by form I mean all that is usually included in style, plus whatever has to do with the sense of something transacting between the book and its reader. Whoever lays hold on the collective mind at the node from which issues the green bough of constructive change, finds himself impelled toward what is later discovered to be the prophetic form. What, after all, is the slow growth of appreciation of a novelist of the first rank, but the simultaneous widening of our social consciousness to a sense of its own direction.

American novelists are often accused of a failure of form. But is this anything more than an admission of failure of access on the part of the critics? Characteristic art form is seldom perfected until the culture of which it is an expression comes to rest. Of all the factors influencing the American novel form, I should expect the necessity, inherent in a democratic society, of conforming more directly, at any given moment, to the *state* of the collective consciousness rather than to its *direction*, to be the determining item. This is what, generally speaking, conditions the indispensable quality of access. Under the democratic condition it can be achieved only by participation. There is no place in the American consciousness for the superior being standing about with his hands in his pockets, "passing remarks."

The democratic novelist must be inside his novel rather than outside in the Victorian fashion of Thackeray or the reforming fashion of Mr. Wells. He may, like Mr. Sherwood Anderson, be so completely inside as to be unclear in his conclusion about the goal, but there he is, Americanly, on his way. The reference of personal conduct to an overhead Judgment which forced the earlier novelist to assume the god in the disposition of his characters, has here given place to a true democratic desire of man to see himself as he is seen by the people with whom he does business. His search is not so much for judgment as for revelation, quick, nervous appreciations of place, relationship and solidarity. But in every case the validity of the American form will rest upon that intuitive access to the collective consciousness, which it is the dream, and probably the mission of democracy to achieve.

NOTES

1. "The Scope of Fiction," *New Republic* 30 (1922): 6.
2. *The American Rhythm: Studies and Reexpressions of Amerindian Songs* (Boston: Houghton, 1930), 19.

"Greatness in Women," appearing in the North American Review *in 1923, explores the problem that Austin had suggested eleven years earlier: "The social ideal, in which I was bred, is the villain of my plot."*[1] *In Austin's view, social conventions had failed to adequately define, recognize, and employ qualities of individual greatness in American women to the extent that they had with regard to men. Austin's view is that most Americans had been taught to value historical figures more than those living in the present and that this makes it difficult to perceive or evaluate qualities of greatness in those living in the present, particularly in women, who have not traditionally been recognized for roles in public life.*

In her essay "American Women and the Intellectual Life," Austin had called for the emergence of "a genuine woman culture" among "determinedly young and preponderately male" American intellectuals.[2] *Here she continues that argument, noting that "objective judgments in respect to what is written or painted or discovered" have been "almost exclusively based on the way the thing has been done by men."*

"Greatness in Women" challenges women to utilize more effectively their unique talents and qualities in the arena of feminist political advocacy. Further, it suggests Austin's belief that American women in the early 1920s had not yet adequately matched their recent political advances, as signaled by the vote, with similarly new and appropriate criteria for leadership and, more broadly, gender identity.

from Greatness in Women

In the recent popular poll for names of greatness, all the categories of greatness as they are recognized among the great seem to have been missed with singular completeness. This was perhaps to be expected in a popular expression in which the great themselves could hardly be invited to participate. There was also to be noticed a curious and informing difference between the lists of the greatest twelve men and similar selections among the names of women. Almost without exception the lists of men were made up from among the names of men admittedly able, and distinguished, by reputation at least, for sustained achievement. But the women's candidates were so generally selected from among the names of those merely prominent, that apparently the only selective principle at work had been the frequency with which those names appeared in the newspapers.

Confirming this impression that American women are without any recognized criterions of superiority in non-feminine achievement, comes the first general election in which the demand for women in public place, which was supposed to be the mainspring of woman suffrage, has had free play, with the result that the only woman in the Senate owes her position to a man's appointment.

Not to know their own prophets is a rather serious predicament for women, who have hoped for the amelioration of social conditions through the interpenetration of the social organism by woman thought. Not to be able to know them is surely culpable. For however much we concede to the inexperience of women in group activity, it remains a fundamental law of human nature that revelation arrives by way of individuals rather than by way of committees. Prophetic inspiration is not to be produced by the accretion of small individual foresights, nor is there any discoverable way of compensating the high seriousness of collective intention for those flashes of illumination which, from the souls of

Originally published in the *North American Review* 217 (1923). Reprinted by permission of the *North American Review*.

the truly great, light up unexpected horizons. America must, if her women are to make a contribution commensurate with the contributions of men, not only produce great women, but also be able to measure and appreciate their greatness in terms of the present hour. It begins to appear to the most hopefully obtuse of feminists that the demand for great place for women gathers little force in the absence of any number of women widely recognized as capable of filling it. . . .

We are already clear on one point, which is that "greatest women" shall be great as women, and not in any sense imitators of men's quality of greatness. This is a way of saying that they must be, in type, maternal. Women's genius may take protean forms, but its mode will be almost universally to seek fulfillment in group service rather than in the personal adventure.

Let me not be understood here as merely setting up the traditional compliment of woman's great altruism. I am speaking of a mode of procedure rather than of moral qualities. So far as this disposition has showed itself, one may count on the fingers of one hand the instances where woman's tendency to group service has served society better, or even as well, as man's genius for personal distinction. What I mean by maternalism in greatness is not so much a question of ethics as of the nature and direction of the feminine drive. To take the field of woman's special "womanly" preeminence, the relief of pain, and conceding the incipience of such conspicuous relief as the field hospital and the Red Cross to women; have they accomplished any more by such measures than the man who discovered the use of chloroform, than Lister and Pasteur and a score of other men working separately, under pressure of ambition, intellectual curiosity or the hope of gain?

Men are often supremely qualified for working with and through the group by ambition, egotism, the will to power. Women are seldom good protagonists within the group; but by virtue of their maternal quality they are more likely to function at their highest only for and on account of the group, with a marked disposition to function more often administratively than constructively. Napoleon, I suppose, is the outstanding male type, enlarging France that he might himself be enlarged as Emperor of it, and Joan of Arc is the type maternal, spending herself that France might be freed. With men the personal relation which is the driving wheel of great careers is so interwoven with the male endowment that it is seldom, even for purposes of classification, to be separated from it. With women the revelation not infrequently transcends the feminine qualification. Thus great women are often accused of being masculine in their time — even Joan suffered under that stigma — and more often than not find it necessary to forego womanly rewards for the sake of maternal achievement.

In women whose genius is not social, the maternal faculty takes the form of that divine givingness without which one may not become great even as a courtesan.

If you think of a great actress, for example, you immediately think of some great actor or playwright to the elucidation of whose genius she devoted her own. If she is a great thinker, like Olive Schreiner or Mary Wollstonecraft, you find her thinking for other women. Always this givingness of great women differs from the givingness of men in being centered on the recipient rather than on the act. Eve, when she had secured the apple, found in the end nothing better to do with it than to give it to a man. Women will die for a faith, for a child or a lover. But men think it more important to die well when it is required of them, than to inquire why so much dying.

This disposition to emphasize the objective of greatness rather than its mode characterizes that other universal concomitant of greatness, as it is exemplified in women, the gift of prophecy. True greatness cannot exist only for the hour. In order to serve it must foresee, and in women, here again perhaps because of long training in the maternal capacity, the gift of prophecy tends to run forward to meet a specific occasion. It is men who make large impersonal claims upon the future of the universe, who write all the Utopias and invent the world machine. The prophecies of women are for the abolition of slavery, the prohibition of alcohol, the elimination of war. As for the great artist woman, depend upon it, she will be found in the last summing up more interested, as Sara Bernhardt is, for example, in making her art contributory than in making it exceptional.

But it is not quite enough for greatness that a woman should be maternal in her quality and prophetic in her modes. She must also be greatly endowed.

It is at this point that the average American feminist fails. She is a poor judge of the personal equipment necessary for a woman who is to adventure successfully in the field of national or world accomplishment. Neither in respect to the work done, nor in the choice of critical substitutes for opinion, is she able in general to justify her preferences on established grounds. . . .

But one of the driving forces of the feminist movement has been the deep-seated opposition of women to the continuing of social control in the hands of political groups, unified and set in motion by the operations of personality. Especially are they opposed to the type of feminine control which is arrived at by the art of producing a given effect upon men. Yet by their failure to provide themselves with some sure way of knowing which women are intrinsically endowed with the qualification for a superior kind of leadership, they find themselves plunged in the alternative of not having any women in situations of pivotal political or intellectual influence. With the ballot in their hands, the influence of American women in international relations, in domestic policies, in education, in literature and the arts and religion and science, is still largely indirect.

There does not appear to be any immediate way out of this predicament. The process of educating even a minority of women to acute, impersonal judgments of natural capacity in other women, will be unavoidably long. Not much help can be expected from men; for though they have worked out an approximate method of arriving at objective judgments in respect to what is written or painted or discovered, their criterions are almost exclusively based on the way the thing has been done by men.

It must be remembered in this connection that though Joan of Arc depended for her following in the French Army on the personal reaction to her spiritual endowment, she was also a great military genius and gave to France the three modern modes of warfare which Napoleon afterward perfected, methodic organization of cavalry, grouping of artillery, and open order of infantry attack. These were things men could understand and honor accordingly.

Women in the arts, and in our institutions of scientific research, agree in insisting that back of the masculine will to power, and every type of professional competition, there is a more serious deterrent to the success of the women greatly and originally endowed. This is the general incapacity of men to recognize original genius when it occurs in a characteristic womanly manner. All testimony of professional women seems to agree on this point, that a woman who does a new thing has to wait much longer for recognition than a man would have waited for precisely the same thing. In view of recent revelations it hardly seems possible to go on charging this condition wholly to the account of masculinity.

Feminists generally are confessing themselves disappointed with the results, in the field of national influences, of their amazingly efficient organizations. Is it not, perhaps, that the very efficiency of such organizations tends to inhibit the expression of the fortunate variations of woman's genius, and let nothing through into the thought stream but the capacity for efficient organization? Long ago men discovered that this, in the absence of individual genius to be forwarded by it, is a sterile capacity indeed.

It is not unlikely that we have women of superlative equality in the United States; equal at least to the superlativeness of our men. What is lacking is some sure method of recognizing and making use of them.

NOTES

1. *A Woman of Genius* (New York: Doubleday, 1912), 461.
2. *Bookman* 53 (1921): 481.

The cultural integrity and economic health of Native Americans were lifelong concerns for Austin. In "The Folly of the Officials," Austin mounts one of her most forceful arguments against what she saw as mistaken U.S. government policy toward Native Americans as well as the racial prejudice on which it was based. Austin's essay was published as a response to an essay, "The Delusion of the Sentimentalists," which appeared immediately before Austin's essay under the heading "Our Indian Problem" and which was written by Flora Warren Seymour, a commissioner of the Bureau of Indian Affairs. The occasion for this published debate was a growing controversy during the early 1920s over the mission and effectiveness of the Bureau of Indian Affairs in "managing" the nation's native population. The "muddle of Pueblo affairs" that Austin mentions refers to the efforts by Austin, John Collier, and other advocates of Indian autonomy to oppose the suppression of Pueblo ceremonial dances and to defeat the Bursum Bill, a piece of legislation that would have allowed for the further transfer of Pueblo land to non-Indian ownership. These events of the 1920s, related to most Americans via lectures and published exchanges such as this one between Austin and Seymour, finally animated a reform movement led by John Collier, who had learned about the Pueblos while visiting the artists' community in Santa Fe. In 1933, Roosevelt named Collier a commissioner of the Bureau of Indian Affairs, and under his direction, the Bureau enacted the Indian Reorganization Act of 1934, which repealed allotment laws and otherwise reversed a fifty-year trend by providing legal means for preserving tribal ownership of land. While they did not see eye-to-eye on everything, Austin and Collier were successful allies during the 1920s.

Austin's point-by-point engagement of Seymour's argument is so thorough that we have a fairly clear impression of Seymour's argument just by reading Austin's rebuttal. Seymour's essay is a combative statement of the assimilationist position. Using to negative effect the stereotype of the lazy, state-supported "rich Indian," Seymour argues that the current situation of Native Americans is not governed by moral issues, but rather simply caused by "an irresistible movement of world population." For Seymour, the demographics allow no room for nostalgia for traditional Indian culture or tribal ownership of land propounded by "well-meaning but ill-advised ladies." Here siding with the Federated Women's Clubs she had sometimes criticized, Austin argues for the integrity and preservation of the "essential quality of the Indian." The trace of Anglo-Saxon bias at work in Austin's essay is not unusual in her discussions of Native Americans, but in spite of an occasional paternalistic tone, arguably a rhetorical strategy *intended to enlist the support of an almost exclusively non-Indian audience, Austin was an enthusiastic, and more importantly, an effective advocate for Native American autonomy from the turn of the century on. Her reference to Native Americans as a "resource," somewhat troubling today, reflects her feeling that non-Indians must incorporate elements of native metaphysics into their own worldviews if America were ever to develop a unique and successful national culture from its roots up.*

The Indian problem is of world dimensions. It is the problem of Canada and of every South American State, it is the chief internal problem of Turkey in Armenia, of Japan in Korea, of England in Egypt and Palestine, of all European powers in Africa. Why should not our country, rich and at peace and crammed full of executive talent, work out a solution of that problem, which we can hold up to the perplexed other nations as a model? It is the growing disposition to turn inward and attack our own problem before we project ourselves into European affairs, much more than it is a disposition to criticise the Indian Bureau that is behind this movement.

To any one at all familiar with the Indian Problem, Mrs. Seymour's discussion of it is of itself a clear exposition of the reason why it has finally become a problem of national importance engaging the acute attention of the more intelligent citizens, and particularly of the three or four million women making up the Federated Women's Clubs. For the first thing that appears in Mrs. Seymour's statement is that she is totally uninformed as to the relation of the thinking citizen to the Indian question, and only shallowly acquainted with the Indian himself.

She begins by assuming that the average citizen derives his information and his accusing attitude toward the Indian Bureau from the reading of *Ramona* written forty years ago by Helen Hunt Jackson. Miss Jackson's publishers could also have told her of another book by the same author, called *A Century of Dishonor*, one of the most shameful records of Bureaucratic inefficiency ever made in this country or any other, and so authoritative that Mrs. Seymour does not even attempt to deny it, being satisfied merely to say that things are different now. It is even possible that she may never have heard it; as she seems not to be familiar with anything more recent than *Ramona*, not even with the hundreds of books and magazine articles on which the de-

Originally published in the *Forum* 71 (1924). Reprinted by permission of the School of American Research.

termination of the American people to reform their Indian policy has been founded.

At any rate, without other reference to the voluminous literature on the subject, she proceeds to suggest a picture of the Indian as formerly existing in a wild state, roaming about in search of berries and wild game, when as every school-boy knows, the whole economic system of the American Colonies was founded on a corn and potato culture which we took over from the Indians and have improved very little since. Also that before the American Colonists could destroy the Five Nations, they had to destroy the walled towns and their granaries, and finally, that the very group of Indians, the New Mexico Puebleños, whose distress precipitated the present crisis, are town builders, having developed a type of architecture which has given its character to one of the two original architectural types originating within the United States.

She is also leaving out of the picture the significant item that the cousins of our native tribes, a few hundred miles to the south had invented the art of writing, one of the two times in the world when this has happened, and had at the time Europe discovered them, devised a calendar for measuring lapsed time by the movements of the stars, superior to the one in use in Europe. This puts the capacity of their racial stock, though delayed in point of evolution, on par with the stocks developing around the Mediterranean. Having thus omitted everything of real importance in describing the Indian as he is, "the favored child of the Nation" the product of "forty years of protecting care" and with the bland inaccuracy of all apologists for the Indian Bureau, suggests that though "you and I have to work for our share of America's riches," the Indian has his handed to him by a too generous paternalism. But again I have to remind Mrs. Seymour that the Pueblo Indians about whom the recent trouble began, have *never at any time in their history received economic assistance from the government*, until last winter, when their lands and waters had been diminished by unlawful encroachments, until it is no longer possible in two or three pueblos to make a living on them. And even then the relief furnished was not all furnished by the Indian

Bureau, but raised by an appeal made by the Indians themselves to the general public.

The Pueblos are, and always have been, self-supporting, self-respecting, self-organized communities, having representative government and producing arts and crafts comparable to any of the peasant arts of Europe. In thus attempting to bring them within the description of wild, seed and game hunting savages, now feeding happily out of the governmental hand, she is probably not trying to falsify the situation. She probably, though she is an Indian Commissioner, doesn't know any better; and that is the first count on which the Bureau of Indian Affairs has recently been publicly arraigned. Its members and apologists show themselves sloppily inaccurate on all points touching the history, the psychology, the racial capacity, and cultural condition of the tribes with whose welfare they have been entrusted, and for which they have been paid.

Having laid down these generally misleading lines of what the Indian is and what we do for him, Mrs. Seymour devotes several paragraphs to a policy of land allotment of which the best she can say is that it is known to have failed, and attempts to perpetuate the legend about the rich Indian who owns a Packard, and farmer Indians living comfortably on rented lands which the government manages for him.

There lies on my desk while I write, a book prepared by G. E. E. Lindquist under the aegis of the Committee of Social and Religious Surveys, called *The Red Man in the United States*, having a commendatory foreword written and signed by Charles H. Burke, Commissioner of Indian Affairs. The book is not written primarily as a study of Indians, but as a study of the progress of Christian Missions among Indians; the idea not being to discover whether we have made the most of our Indians for our own welfare and for theirs, but to what extent we have made Presbyterians and Baptists and Methodists of them. The primary assumption of this book is that to become a member of one of these sects is the most important thing that could happen to any Indian. Criticism of our Indian policy is therefore confined to those things which would interfere with the missionary objective. And even on this meagre ground of health and food and housing, the book utterly overthrows the rosy picture of present Indian prospects as drawn by Mrs. Seymour.

Concerning the rich Indians with Packards, Mr. Lindquist says: "the recent legend of the rich Indian is a gross exaggeration . . . a former Superintendent of the Union Agency is responsible for the statement that no more than one hundred adults . . . are receiving an income from royalties exceeding $3,000 a year. Possibly not more than a score of these can rightly be termed 'rich Indians.'"

Of the policy of land leasing he says: "unscrupulous white men after an initial payment have refused . . . to make further remittances and continue to live indefinitely rent free on the lands of the Indians." Of the Mississippi Choctaws Lindquist says: "The system is one of peonage!" Of the Omahas one of the outstanding examples of the allotment system he says: "the situation is likely to become serious . . . veneral disease affects 80 to 85 per cent, tuberculosis 25 per cent, trachoma 65 per cent. Of the Mexcalero Apache, 70 per cent have trachoma and 25 per cent are tubercular. Of the tribes that are wholly self-supporting many are mentioned but even they are visited by the white man's dread diseases. When you recall that untended trachoma ends in blindness and that Indian villages with 70 per cent of tuberculosis and 25 per cent of venereal disease are nothing but plague spots to the neighboring white communities, you will begin to see that the revolt of the American people against the inefficiency of our Indian Bureau has more of common sense and less of hysteria in it than Mrs. Seymour supposes. Again, in this book to which the Indian Commissioner has written the preface, occur such statements as this about the Blackfeet: "poverty is almost universal . . . an unfortunate feature is the exploitation to which Indians are subject."

Of the stupidities and absurdities of Indian Education (with the waste of the Indian's time and our money) I would be disposed to say little because the more intelligent Indian officials are themselves beginning to suspect that to bring up an Indian child far from his parents in a steam-heated and electrically equipped boarding school, teaching him, or her to set type or make Irish crochet, is not a very good preparation for living a happy useful life in a Navajo Hogan or a log hut in a Minnesota woods. But Mrs. Seymour seems to make such a point of the happy fortune of the Indian child, that it seems necessary to explain that of the trades taught him, nineteen out of every twenty necessitate his leaving his own home, his kin and kind, and living as a social outcast and an economic drifter on the fringes of white life. The whole tendency of Indian Education as now practiced is to destroy the essential quality of the Indian and to make something out of him of rather less social and economic account than we get in shoals at Ellis Island every day in the year.

Mrs. Seymour admits the hopeless legal tangles of Indian affairs, the dreary and discreditable muddle of them in the hands of the Bureau which has undertaken to manage them. She outlines slightly the muddle of Pueblo affairs which brought on the recent severe criticism of the Indian Bureau. It is true that a part of this muddle is inherited from the Spanish-Mexican regime, and was never cleared up as it should have been; but she fails to state clearly that a good half of the difficulty was initiated *after* the Pueblos fell into our hands, and *while officials of the Indian Bureau were drawing* salaries for the ostensible purpose of correcting such errors and preventing their recurrence....

The problem of the Indian is not for political appointees and civil service clerks, it is for specialists; specialists in public health, in tribal economics, in education. Above everything else it calls for specialists in the subtle and intricate relations that may arise between great forward moving nations and the small backward people incorporated in their midst.

Another factor that the Indian Bureau has utterly failed to reckon with, is the rapidly growing appreciation of such Indian culture as remains to us, as a National Asset having something the same valuation as the big trees of California and the geysers and buffaloes of Yellowstone. The war, which set hundreds of thousands of Americans to touring their native land, went far toward teaching them that in Indian life we have a precious heritage of enjoyment, and of access to forms of culture rapidly disappearing from the earth, superior to anything the rest of the world has to offer. And in the same breath we learned that the present policy of the Indian Bureau is wiping all this out in a dull smear of ugly and ineffectual imitation of white life. That the Bureau has remained utterly obtuse to this alteration of public sentiment is proved by the order issued while the Bureau was under fire about the Pueblo problem, recommending and threatening to do more than recommend the elimination of Indian dances, which met such a storm of public disapproval that by the time it reached them from Washington, a good many Indian agents had to discount the order as they communicated it to the Indians.

This, in fine, is what the Women's Clubs and associated organizations want; an Indian policy which can at least serve as a starter for a world policy toward backward, dependent peoples. A policy which will insure to us the best that the Indian has to give, in place of a policy which forces upon him the worst that we have. A policy of public health which will reasonably secure us against contamination from disease in our contact with our Indian neighbors. A policy of education which will give the Indian reasonable use of himself and his native faculties in the pursuit of life and happiness. And we want this policy in the hands of a group of properly qualified people who will remember that the Indians do not belong to them, but to us, and will hold themselves reasonably sensitive to public opinion on the subject. In so far as the program and personnel of the present Indian Bureau conforms to this general outline, it has nothing to fear, Secretary Work has already shown himself amenable to such specialized information and opinion as the friends of the Indian have furnished him, notably in the case of the Palm Springs Indians in California. That something equally just can be worked out in New Mexico seems more than likely, but this much at least is certain, it will take its initiation where all movements of this kind should originate — in the public consciousness.

NOTES

1. "The Delusion of the Sentimentalists," *Forum* 71 (1924): 278.
2. 277.

Austin had already cracked the market of the New Republic with such pieces as "The American Form of the Novel" (1922) and "The Sense of Humor in Women" (1924) when her essay "The Town That Doesn't Want a Chautauqua" appeared. With Edmond Wilson newly aboard as a contributing editor, Austin's critique of middle-class Chautauqua culture found ready editorial acceptance. Here aligning herself with the "highbrows" against the circuit Chautauqua movement of adult education, already after its peak year in 1924 in what would turn out to be a gradual decline, Austin argues that the cultural uplift of the Chautauqua is superficial and derivative in comparison to genuine creativity and enlightened late-progressive thinking.

It is clearly the vision of America's betterment offered in the salon of Mabel Dodge Luhan in New York that underlies Austin's thinking here. There, absorbing the spirit of both Greenwich Village aestheticism and radical Masses-variety politics, Austin began to articulate her own sense of the limitations of Chautauqua education, joining her voice with that of antibourgeois liberalism as a whole in its critique of what Ford Madox Ford called "Middle Westishness," "a middle-class metaphor, of conventions, piety and hypocrisy."[1]

Austin felt that in addition to the attraction of New Mexico's creative artists and writers colonies, Santa Fe — with its rich mixture of indigenous New Mexican influences — provided its own authentic cultural environment without the thin overlay of imposed lyceum enrichment. She observes that in addition to having the company of "people of the first rank of creative and intellectual achievement" in New Mexico, "there is the relief of unusual entertainment, so often lacking in the American small town; the pageantry of the Indian dance-drama, the Spanish fiesta, the open rituals of the Church and picturesque survivals."[2] Austin implies that even if the Chautauqua might play well in the small college towns of the Midwest, in the exotic environment of Santa Fe, by its very nature on the edge of the American mainstream, it was simply superfluous. Santa Fe is, in Austin's mind, plainly not Carl Van Vechten's Maple Valley, Iowa, nor even Zona Gale's Portage, Wisconsin. It is a city refusing to subscribe to what she would later call "that furious obsession of alikeness which has expressed itself in our culture through the medium of the Lyceum, the Chautauqua, and the Outline-Story."[3]

The Town That Doesn't Want a Chautauqua

New York is accustomed to thinking itself the capital of creative effort in the Americas, having drawn to it the most representative minds of the generation which has charged itself, in the spirit of a crusade, with the fight for the freedom of the creative spirit. But during the past month, New York has given place to an older capital, and a newer expeditionary advance against the banners of Main Street. It is at Santa Fe, the oldest self-established capital in the New World, still the capital of New Mexico, and the most European of towns in all that meets the eye, since its oldness is more in evidence than its newness, that the battle is staged.

The streets of Santa Fe are narrow, its gardens walled, its houses still predominately an undivided item of the brown soil and flat-topped mesas. Its population is 40 percent Spanish-speaking; its hours ring to soft cathedral chimes: religious processions still wind along its kindly streets, and guitars make musical its summer dusk. Also it has a Rotary Club, Kiwanis and Women's Clubs and a Chamber of Commerce, and the largest and most important group of creative workers, painters, poets, novelists, etchers, sculptors, architects, between the Mississippi and the Pacific coast. Mediating these diverse elements of population is a considerable contingent of people rather above the average for towns of the size of Santa Fe, drawn there by the climate, by the charm of its old world atmosphere, and by the fact that Santa Fe really is the capital of creative and intellectual effort in the western half of the continent. Not only are distinguished visitors continuously passing and repassing Santa Fe, but workers in many fields of research, such as the country naturally calls for, archaeology, ethnology, geology and aboriginal literature, make it from time to time the headquarters of their work. It is quite possible — in addition to the residents — for such diverse and compelling personalities as Sinclair Lewis, John Galsworthy, Spinden and Morley of the Mayan expedition, John Sloan

Originally published in *New Republic* 47 (1926). Reprinted by permission of the School of American Research.

and Alfred Kreymborg to be in Santa Fe at one time or within a few weeks of each other. Or it might be Willa Cather, Harrington the Indian language expert, Old Bill White, Anne Martin the feminist, Alma Gluck and Robert Henri. Any town and its inhabitants, worth being visited by such distinguished people, is bound in the course of time to produce something worth watching, and eventually profitable to the community at large. What Santa Fe is producing at the moment is a dramatic clash between the creative type of mind and interest, and the type most accurately described as the Chautauqua-minded.

That institution known as the Chautauqua Circuit is a pure American product, the outstanding characterization of our naive belief and our superb faith that culture can, like other appurtenances of democracy, proceed by majorities. As the Chautauqua stood during the last quarter of the last century, it was a really important instrument of adult education. It took the whole intellectual product of the period, decanted and distributed it with sincerity and skill. Nor does it appear that the originators of the Chautauqua idea ever mistook the nature either of their intention or their achievement. But the beneficiaries of it did. By the beginning of the present century the pleasant air diffused by lectures and superficial predigested study courses and the presence on platforms of distinguished personalities politely stepping down the results of their labor to the comprehension of unlaboring audiences, had produced in those audiences the still more pleasing illusion of actually having what they had only heard about. Just as anybody today who can without actual damage to himself pull a lever, punch a button, or uncover his arm to a serum syringe thinks of himself as participation in the age of science, so the million faithful attendants at study clubs, at Circles and Lecture programs have come to feel a proprietary interest in the prevailing "culture" of their age. It is this primary illusion which is back of unspecialized attempts to award merit or blame in American art and thought by censoring the product. The motives for such attempted censorship are neither so puritanical nor so Freudian as are generally assumed by the generation which suffers most. Reason enough can be found in the fact that no single circumstance in American life is calculated to undeceive the Chautauqua-minded as to the quality of that "culture" which has been doled out to them under the foremost names and the best auspices. There can be no doubt that a vast majority of Americans, particularly American women, sincerely suppose that "culture" is generated in "courses," and proceeds as by nature from the lecture platform. The general disrespect in which the "business" sense of the creative worker is held in the United States would prevent any contrary idea from gaining ground; so that the driving out of a resident community of creative workers of established reputation by a Chautauqua summer colony would inevitably seem to many people a great cultural gain.

So much is necessary, by way of explanation of what happened at Santa Fe. Unique as that little city is, it is still sufficiently American to have produced a group to whom a summer Chautauqua on its border seemed a valid way of raising the cultural tone of the community, while at the same time it produces that great American desideratum of "bringing money into the town."

What more natural than that a group of Texas club women who have for the last year been looking for a site for a Chautauqua as a centre for the Federated Clubs of the nine Southwestern states, should have been attracted to Santa Fe, and in the complete sincerity of their acceptance of the democratization of "culture," should have ignored to the point of actually convincing themselves that it did not exist, the protest of any Santa Feans who failed to agree with them. Without any underthought the project was nominated a "cultural colony," and the universal reaction of other towns in the district to the rapidly developing objections of the ignored creative elements of the population, was that they had suddenly gone "plumb crazy." That was to be expected from painters, poets and such like producers of the raw stuff of culture, but — and this is unique in the history of American culture — an important contingent of the "businessmen," doctors, lawyers, merchants, educators, at Santa Fe were promptly found to be possessed of the heresy that maintaining a creative atmosphere is sometimes more important than "bringing money into the town," and that a creative type of culture is a better thing for the community as a whole, a better contribution to the future of the state, than a Chautauqua type. This decision, reached almost by instinct by a significant minority of the ancient desert capital, with neither drum nor bush, suddenly showed itself as the sharp edge of a sword dividing the ways of community thought.

It has become a convention to speak of the most frequently deplored traits of our American culture as Middle-Western. What we mean is that most American communities established in the last half-century have not so much grown as been builded, subject to a notion of "the good life" as it was conceived along the Ohio and upper Mississippi valleys, a notion that overflowed into the West and achieved itself, largely by means of Chautauqua devices, without producing the satisfactions expected of it. Never has a cultural idea so quickly reached its apogee and so soon resolved into a secret dismay. Not only have enterprises for the expression of gregariousness in a cultural guise disappeared from uncounted towns, but the towns themselves are now doing their best to look as if they never had them. All over the West there is a fumbling movement toward a culture rooted in the living processes of community life, but nowhere a formulated program, scarcely an articulate choice. Possibly because the Chautauqua type of cultural endeavor has proceeded from the very sources from which true culture is conventionally supposed to be derived, from the social activities for which "our best women" are sponsors, there has been a marked reluctance of definition, and no explicit rejections. Probably no other town of its size in the Southwest, however much private citizens might have deplored it, would have flouted the convention that a Women's Club "culture colony" is inevitably a cultural advantage and a financial gain. Suddenly like a flashing sword out of the ancient city of the Holy Faith came both choice and definition.

There are, said Santa Fe, two types of cultural centre, the creative and the Chautauqua, and the two are incompatible in the same community. Having one, we prefer not to have the other. Even more startling, the first pronouncement of the group that called itself the Old Santa Fe Association, was put forth in a manner that placed the artist on the same footing as a business man, that came near to the unprecedented heresy of assuming that an artist *is* a business man. To prove it, the local paper issued a long list of artists of every description resident at Santa Fe, with their properties and incomes, in which astonishingly many of them were shown to be "solid" citizens as though they had been members of the Chamber of Commerce, as in fact a score of the protestants proved to be. The hush that fell upon the whole nine states known as the Southwest, following this announcement, was thick enough to have been cut with the proverbial knife.

What did cut it was the trenchant response of New York, for the protestants numbered several members whose "business" of influencing opinion was on a scale that, applied to selling worsted yarn or hardware would have been called "big." Not only the metropolitan press was stirred, but weekly magazines, followed by the newspapers of the inland cities, working westward until comment and approval penetrated the mazed borders of New Mexico. Whatever discovery Santa Fe had made for itself, it proved, like so many discoveries, to be the unvoiced conviction of innumerable other small cities and large. There are two types of community culture, one in which the community works by individuals to produce definite achievement on a cultural plane, and the other in which the community exists chiefly to hear about what has been produced. And even the towns which, if put to the test, might vote for the more popular and populous type, are agreed that it would be a relief to know that there is one town, preferably Santa Fe, made safe against it.

To have this out, all set down in uncontrovertible print, is itself a great gain in the evolution of community life in the United States. To admit that there is a creative life, not incompatible with the ordinary life of druggists and hardware merchants, doctors and lawyers — such a pleasant and productive life as is now being lived at Santa Fe — and yet clearly stated as incompatible with much that calls itself "culture," is a gain that might not have been made elsewhere in this generation. Beside this gain, the insistence of the originating group, that in spite of the widely stated objections they mean to go as far as they can in superimposing their Chautauqua-mindedness upon Santa Fe, though it may seriously disturb the civic equilibrium of old Santa Fe, is, by its betrayal of the lack of a saving grace of humor, robbed of all its dignity and half its power to offend. "Culture" has often been made absurd by its devotees in America, but never before so without a savor of gallantry. And always there is the possibility that the majority of the General Federation of Women's Clubs — which as an institution has never quite lacked worldly penetration as to its own place in the American scheme — may not feel itself so necessitous in the matter that it must make a cuckoo's nest of the most distinctive and creatively distinguished town in the Southwest, to incubate its own cultural expression. Any number of towns are open to them with undivided welcome and an unaffected allegiance to the Chautauqua type of summer colony, still serviceable where the conditions favor it.

There is another aspect of the situation in New Mexico of an even profounder and more revealing significance in its relation to the problem of American culture as a whole. The native, Spanish-speaking population, descendants of our Spanish colonial families, have expressed themselves more definitely on the subject of the proposed "culture colony" than upon any cultural problem since the American occupation. Courteously but firmly, and with a thoroughly Latin capacity for expressing more than they have said, El Centro de Cultura and El Union Protectiva have added themselves to the numerical majority of protestants. Up to the time that the project was prematurely announced as an accomplished fact, it had occurred to nobody to ask whether the Spanish colonials, whose cultural status has for a hundred years been that of a conquered people, had anything to say to this second invasion. During which time it has been forgotten that this people came to New Mexico out of the siglo de oro that produced Lope de Vega, Calderon, the Escurial, grand opera and the novel, all the golden century of Spain. Seeds like that can lie in a racial strain a long time, and then put forth, as here in New Mexico they are beginning to do, signs of self-rooted cultural life. Today there is among the descendants of these oldest American families more of the kind of expression that is called "folk art" than in any indigenous group within the United States. Wouldn't it be just that dramatic value which the invisible History Maker loves, if this reviving root of one of the world's great ages of cultural advance should be the point on which our most purposefully cultural institution snags? Wouldn't it somehow take the wind out of a few bubbles that float red, white and blue on the surface of our national expression?

There is no doubt that the Chautauqua as an institution has a legitimate, even an honored place in our cultural evolution. But it belongs to and legitimately ends with the era of its distinguished culture hero, William Jennings Bryan. Probably its best service will prove to be the evidence it affords that its characteristic product, the Chautauqua mind, is not the material out of which golden centuries are made. And in the meantime Santa Fe adds to its uniqueness of joyous adventure by becoming the town that wouldn't have a Chautauqua.

NOTES

1. Qtd. in Frederick J. Hoffman, *The 20s* (1949; reprint, New York: Free Press-Macmillan, 1962), 369.
2. "Why I Live in Santa Fe," *Goldenbook* 16 (1932): 307.
3. "Folk Literature," *Saturday Review of Literature* 11 Aug. 1928: 34.

"Woman Alone" appeared in The Nation in 1927 as the ninth in a series of anonymous articles "giving the personal backgrounds of women with a modern point of view."[1] This autobiographical essay gives an important and focused look at the early development of Austin's thinking, particularly concerning her sense of identity as a woman and her self-consciously "radical" sense of gender conflict.

In contrast to her 1932 book-length autobiography Earth Horizon, written largely from a third person point of view about "Mary," "Woman Alone" reveals Austin in a significantly more personal and familiar voice, even as she insists on the need of women for "detachment from the personal issue" in their relationships with men. In addition, Austin's sense of an "inherency of design"[2] in the pattern of her life and its narrative, which she describes in some detail in Earth Horizon, is also suggested here in the very specific terms of the evolution and determinancy of her feminism.

Woman Alone

The founder of my mother's family came across with Lafayette and married a Massachusetts farmer's daughter with a tradition of Indian blood. By successive removals the family pioneered into Pennsylvania, the Ohio Valley, and the prairies of Illinois. There, in 1861, my mother married a young Englishman who had just won his captaincy in the first three months of the Civil War. A few years after the close of the war I was born as the third of six children. My mother's people were mostly farming folk, though my father was admitted to the bar; he died when I was about ten, of a long-drawn-out war disability. None of the family attained any distinction beyond that of being — the men, good fighters, and the women, notable housewives, rather more forceful and inventive than the men. To account for myself, who turned out to be that blackest of black sheep to a Middle Western family, a radical-minded literary artist, I can record only that my grandfather played the flute and that a member of the French collateral branch was distinguished as a physicist and chemist.

I scarcely know why my being a radical should have proved such a cross to the rest of the family, since they were themselves shouting Methodists, black Abolitionists — my grandfather was known to have entertained Negroes at his table — and my mother a suffragist and an ardent member of the W. C. T. U., which at that time represented the most advanced social thinking among women, saving itself from ostracism only by remaining well within the orthodox religions and confining its activities to moral crusades. There were also "purity leagues" for achieving a single standard of sex behavior, and in connection with the temperance movement what would now be called "eugenic" propaganda, though that word had not then come into use. My mother saw to it that I read the pamphlets and heard the lectures pertaining to all these matters, without in the least realizing that she was thus preparing me for a radical career. I personally "sat under" Susan B. Anthony, Frances Willard, and Anna Shaw.

Reprinted from *The Nation* magazine, 124 (1927). © The Nation Company, Inc.

With this background it was inevitable that I should become a fighting feminist. But I cannot make clear my approach and method in regard to this problem of my generation without describing my own position in the family as an unwanted, a personally resented child. Probably few families in that age of enforced maternity were without some such member; but in fewer still did the intrusion take on such proportions of offense. Not that I ever blamed my mother, when I came to know them, for not wanting a child under the circumstances to which I was born. Nor do I, sorely as it hurt at the time, any longer resent that I should so early and so sharply have had my status as alien and intruder forced upon me. As you will see, it was my poor mother who lost the most in the conflict of irreconcilable temperaments never modulated by personal sympathy. Could she possibly have anticipated that I should end by being included in a list of prominent feminists, nothing would have pleased her so much; the trouble was that with that terrible pre-natal bias between us, she could never by any whipping-up of a sense of duty grow to like me, and the rest of the family took its tone from her. Long before I came to an intellectual understanding of the situation I had accepted as fact that I was not liked and could not expect the normal concessions of affection. By that adaptive instinct which still intolerably wrings my heart when I see it operating in young children, I had learned that it was only by pushing aside all considerations of liking and insisting on whatever fundamental rightness inhered in a particular situation, that I could secure a kind of factual substitute for family feeling and fair play. This began so early that though I can recall many occasions of mystified hurt at being rebuffed in the instinctive child's appeal, I can recall no time in which I did not have to conceal that hurt in order to bring all a child's wit and intelligence to bear on making good my right to be treated, factually at least, as a lawful member of the family. Out of this I developed very early an uncanny penetration into the fundamental ethics of personal situations which my mother was too just to refuse and not always clever enough to evade. By the time I was old enough to discuss our relationships with my mother the disposition to seek for logical rather than emotional elements had become so fixed that I had even made myself believe that being liked was not important. I had, at least, learned to do without it.

All this must be told in order that the bias and the method of my feminism may be understood. For life played an ironic trick on my mother. The pretty and darling daughters were taken away, and only the unwished-for ugly duckling left, between the oldest and the youngest sons. As if this were not enough, by the time the elder son was ripe for college there began to be signs that the daughter and not the son was the clever one. After my father's death my mother's affectional interests, as is often the case with widows, gathered and intensified around my older brother, who proved a good son and a good citizen, but without any distinguishing gifts. When in college he had, chiefly I suspect in response to my mother's passionate wish, displayed literary and forensic tastes which he was unable to support without liberal contributions from mother and sister. These he accepted at first gingerly, and finally with such freedom that many a theme, many a quip and paragraph which appeared in the college journal over his name had been wrung out of me by such concessions as sisters do to this day obtain from older brothers by ministering to masculine complacency. Although my mother was often a party to our traffic and occasional squabbles over it, she was always able, when the things appeared, to accept them as evidence of what she so much wished. After her death I found a scrapbook in which they were all carefully arranged with my brother's name in her handwriting underneath. And lest any of the generation for whom the woman's right to the product of her own talent is completely established should think this an unusual situation, I recommend the reading of the current if out-moded novels of that period, such, for example, as the novels of Madame Sarah Grand or May Sinclair's "Mary Olivier." For the greater part of the nineteenth century, in fact, it was not only usual but proper for parents openly to deplore that the sons had not inherited talents inconveniently bestowed upon the daughters.

I seem always to have known that I would write. Probably there was evidence of my having the necessary endowment, had there been anybody able to recognize literary talent, or tell me what to do about it. The attitude of the family was crushing.

"What makes you think *you* can write?" In truth, I did not know. Looking back on the idea of a literary career which prevailed in the Middle West of that period, it was probably as well for me that nobody knew. I won a college degree by dint of insisting on it, and by crowding its four years into two and a half. My brother had a full four years. That I got so much was partly a concession to the necessity of my earning a living. With the college education I could teach, and teaching was regarded then as a liberal profession, eminently suited to women. Being plain and a little "queer," it was hoped rather than expected that I would marry. My queerness consisted, at that time, in entertaining some of the ideas that have got me elected to this list, in stoutly maintaining against all contrary opinion that I would some day write, and in the — to my family — wholly inexplicable habit of resting my case on its inherent rightness rather than upon the emotional reactions it gave rise to.

The summer I was out of college my mother decided to go West with my brother, so that he might "take up land" and grow with the country, taking me with her as being still too young for self-support. No use inquiring now whether this was a good move for me. Before the Pacific Coast filled up with Middle Westerners it was gorgeous, an exciting place to be. Probably it proved a retardation of my literary career and a stimulus to radicalism. The immediate result was that I married. My mother had sunk all her little capital in giving my brother his start; there was no place in the home for me, and no money to prepare me for any happy way of supporting myself. I taught a couple of years, not very successfully. And, anyway, I wished to be married. Contrary to the popular conception about literary women, I like domestic life and have a genuine flair for cooking. And I wanted children profoundly.

I still intended to write, but never in my life having met a professional literary person there was no one to tell me that the two things were incompatible. Under ordinary circumstances they are not. What I did not in the least realize was that the circumstances were not ordinary. I married a man with social and educational background not unlike my own; a man I could thoroughly respect for his personal quality, quite apart from any achievement. There seemed no reason why, had I been what I appeared to my family, and to my husband no doubt, the marriage should not have proved successful in every particular. What I appeared was an average young person, clever and a little odd, but not so odd that a house to keep and a baby every two years wouldn't restore me to entire normality. True, my health was not good. All my mother's babies had been sickly; I as the sickliest had always been the first to "catch" every childish ailment, and as it was not the custom in those days to send for the doctor until you knew what was the matter with the patient I seldom received medical attention. But no one had ever suggested that this need interfere with marriage and having children. It was a superstition left over from my mother's generation that ill health in women was cured by having children. Nor did I realize how compelling the creative urge would become in me. Had I even suspected it I would not have supposed it a bar to marriage. I thought that two intelligent young people could do about as they liked with life. But, like myself, my young husband was without preparation for maintaining a household. At the end of twelve years we were still living in a town of about 300 inhabitants on an income inadequate to reasonable comfort, with an invalid child.

My first baby came in the second year and left me a tortured wreck. I know now that I did not have proper medical treatment, but at the time nothing much was thought of such things. My memory of the first seven or eight years of marriage is like some poor martyr's memory of the wheel and the rack, all the best things of marriage obscured by a fog of drudgery impossible to be met and by recurrent physical anguish. For before I had discovered the worst that had happened to me I had tried a second time to have a child, unsuccessfully. Brought up as I was, in possession of what passed for eugenic knowledge, it had never occurred to me that the man I had married would be less frank about his own inheritance than I had been about mine — much to his embarrassment, for nice girls were seldom frank at that time. I who had entered motherhood with the highest hopes and intentions had to learn too late that I had borne a child with tainted blood. I had to find it all out by myself. My husband's family exchanged glances, and remained silent. My mother said:

"I don't know what you have done, daughter, to have such a judgment upon you." But I, brutally and indelicately, as I was given to understand, insisted upon uncovering family history until I found out. I said to my husband: "Why did you never tell me?" He said: "Because it never occurred to me." At home, he told me, they were all brought up never to refer to the obvious handicap. That was the well-bred Christian way of the 1890's. As for my own family, from beginning to end they never ceased to treat me as under a deserved chastisement.

In a way this tragic end of my most feminine adventure brought the fulfillment of my creative desire, which had begun to be an added torment by repression. Caring for a hopelessly invalid child is an expensive business. I had to write to make money. In the end I was compelled to put my child in a private institution where she was happier and better cared for than I could otherwise manage. My husband's family were good sports. They never forgot the birthdays and Christmases, and the probability that there might be normal human reactions. To my own family who demanded somewhat accusingly what they should say, I said: "You can say I have lost her." Which was true and a great relief to them. My mother died shortly after, but was never quite reconciled to my refusal to accept my trouble as a clear sign of God's displeasure. So for sixteen years.

Released thus to the larger life which opened to me with literary success, I found plenty of reason for being a feminist in the injustices and impositions endured by women under the general idea of their intellectual inferiority to men. What I have just related are the facts that gave color and direction to my feminist activities. But I must go back a little to explain the kind of thing that got me called a radical, which was not what is called radical today. I was neither a Bolshevik nor a Communist, not even a Socialist or free lover. I thought much that was said at the time about Home and Mother, sentimental tosh; I thought it penalized married love too much to constitute the man she loved the woman's whole horizon, intellectual, moral, and economic. I thought women should be free to make their contribution to society by any talent with which they found themselves endowed, and be paid for it at rates equal to the pay of men. I thought everything worth experiencing was worth talking about; I inquired freely into all sorts of subjects. I got myself read out of the Methodist church by organizing, along in the nineties, the first self-conscious enterprise of what has been called the Little Theater movement and acting in its plays. Worst of all, I talked freely of art as though it had a vital connection with living. One example of the sort of reactions an unbridled radical such as I was had to face must suffice. That was the beginning of various movements for applying the social wisdom of the more fortunate classes to the problems of the underprivileged — juvenile courts, probation officers, big brother and sister associations, and in particular, the activity finally objectified as the court of domestic relations, in which I was particularly interested. I had spoken freely and publicly about the necessity of bringing those unlearned in life into more or less compulsory compliance with our best experience. Just why this should figure as an offense to anybody I am still at a loss to know; but the next time I went to my mother's house, I discovered that there had been a family council, and it was put to me that, while the family did not attempt to dictate what I should say away from the neighborhood of the family, I must understand that in that neighborhood and especially under the family roof I must refrain from all mention of so objectionable a subject as public remedies for private relations, or find my mother's door forever closed to me. Not a word, you see, about the incredible private tragedy which had come to me for lack of a public remedy! . . . Oh yes, I took it, standing, for the same reason that I took it the day my pretty young sister was buried and my mother flung away from me and cried aloud on God for taking Jenny and leaving me. It wasn't until I caught the family — what was left of it — trying to put over on the younger generation the same repressions and limitations they had practiced upon me that I blew up. Suddenly I found the younger generation on my side.

As for not being under the necessity of being liked, which began as a defense, it has become part of my life philosophy. I see now that too many of the impositions of society upon women have come of their fear of not being liked. Under disguising names of womanliness, of tact, of religion even, this humiliating necessity, this compulsive fear goes through all social use like mould, corrupting the bread of life. It is this weakness of women displayed toward their sons which has fostered the demanding attitude of men toward them. It puts women as a class forever at the mercy of an infantile expectation grown into an adult convention. So I have made a practice of standing out against male assumption of every sort, especially their assumption of the importance of masculine disapproval — more than anything else against their assumption that they have a right to be "managed." But it is the women I am aiming at, women and their need for detachment from the personal issue. At present the price for refusing to "manage" men is high, but not too high for a self-respecting woman to pay.

NOTES

1. "These Modern Women," *Nation* 124 (1927): 228.
2. *Earth Horizon* (1932; reprint, Albuquerque: Univ. of New Mexico Press, 1991), vii.

"How I Found the Thing Worth Waiting For" is one of Austin's most engaging and far-ranging pieces of social commentary. Drawing upon her own early contacts with feminism and women's issues and speaking from the point of view of what she calls the "Stone Age," a perspective arising from her contact with Native Americans, Austin mounts a broad critique of business, "SatEvePost Culture," and contemporary radicalism.

A clear alternative vision of an ideal America, however, is somewhat distant here, obscured in the loping, transitional style that at times emerges in her work. The rhetoric is almost oratorical in its manner, reflecting perhaps Austin's own intense involvement with public speaking at the time. As the article appeared, Austin was in the middle of one of the most extended and exhausting lecture tours of her career, traveling throughout the East, speaking for $100 or $150 an engagement and giving up 25 percent of that to her booking agencies. National and modernist in her scope, projecting the growth of a new "spiritual approach to economic solutions" and the rise of "group consciousness" among Americans, Austin argues for "communicability," for the development of a new vocabulary to express the evolution of public life. Her call upon the "intelligentsia" she criticizes to provide her with such a vocabulary is only partly ironic, as is, in a different way, the title of the essay. "How I Found the Thing Worth Waiting For" is less about the end of the road than it is about the ongoing process of developing ideas by communicating them, a process Austin was actively pursuing at the time. Included here is the first third of the essay.

from How I Found the Thing Worth Waiting For

When I consider my beginnings I see that I must have been born a radical, in the sense of never being willing to accept what was told me, of wanting always to go to the roots of things. I recall my earliest expression of it, when I was full of pride in my first five dollars which my grandfather had given me for reading the Bible from cover to cover. I was then about ten years old — if a child of mine had to read the Old Testament I would prefer that it should be before the reader was old enough to know what it meant — and I asked my mother how it was they knew that the Bible was the Inspired Word of God. "Because it says in the bible that it is God's Word," my mother answered. But the germs of literary criticism must also have been in me, for I recall replying that not everything in books was necessarily true, since in Hans Christian Anderson it said . . . "But if it is God's word it must be true," my mother placidly insisted.

"There now," said my father, with that odd burr in his speech which only came there when he was amused, "let's see ye get to the bottom of that, ye little . . . " but I never can be sure of the quaint Scotch words that he used to apply to me more than to any of his other children.

FEMINISM BY INHERITANCE

The beginnings of feminism must also have come to me by inheritance, since I can never recall a single incident that was told me about my revolutionary and pioneering ancestry, that did not revolve about my great and greater grandmothers. There was a tale about Grandmother Graham that I particularly liked: how shortly after their marriage my grandfather who, because he was lame, had been apprenticed to a tailor before he made a chemist of himself, had bought a fine piece of cloth and made up for her

Originally published in Survey 61 (1929). Reprinted by permission of the School of American Research.

the first ladies' tailored suit ever seen in our town. Afterward he had her daguerreotype taken in it, over which the town was so exercised that the clergyman gave out that he would preach a sermon against female vanity; which was a pleasant custom of the Methodists of that day. It wasn't really vanity that was back of the daguerreotype, but a kind of tribal loyalty. The family name on the maternal side was Daguerre — Middlewesternized to Dugger — and it was believed that the man who had caught the sun in his snare was of a collateral branch.

What I liked best about the story was that, on the day of the reproving sermon, grandmother sailed down the aisle to hear it *dressed in her tailored gown.* Well, her mother had distinguished herself by persuading Greatgrandfather Dugger to put in a water wheel, and herself invited the neighbor women to set up their spinning wheels in the barn loft, to be run by water power. Nothing saved the situation from complete condemnation except that the women actually did spin more yarn on the water-turned wheels. On such excerpts from the family saga I was brought up.

After my father's death, my mother, to fill the gaping days, "turned temp'rance," and was eventually swept into the devoted train of Frances Willard. Frances Willard had a charm under her tongue which could have wiled a bird off a bush; she also succeeded in being a ramping radical without her small-town, Protestant, Middlewestern following ever finding it out. Besides prohibition, she had the most revolutionary ideas about marriage and politics, about the place of women in the scheme of things. Every now and then I can trace ideas of mine which are still too new to be borne by our intelligentsia, as logical developments from the W. C. T. U. pamphlets which my mother used to give me.

This is not the place to explain fully why prohibition was the only idea which ever "took," among Miss Willard's worshipful disciples. Partly because she traced most of the evils she attacked to drink, and partly because the doing away with drink was a plain objective goal at which her followers hoped in their lifetime to arrive. Also because the women who followed her were of an age to be already settled in their chosen moralistic behaviors. They were revolutionary only in their thoughts.

Later I was to suffer much at the hands of my family for my logical evolution in behavior along the lines indicated by Frances Willard. In the late eighties and the nineties, my poor mother often wondered what she had done that Providence should have given her a daughter who departed so far from what a well-brought-up young Methodist young woman should be. When I was speaking publicly, among the earliest to espouse the idea of what afterward became the Court of Domestic Relations (only I wished it to be not a court, but a bureau or commission — some device for putting the wisdom of the more experienced members of society to the service of the less experienced in managing their domestic relations), after a family council I was advised by my elder brother that, although the family would not attempt to control what I said outside, I must understand that such ideas as mine must never be mentioned under my mother's roof, under penalty of my finding her doors forever closed to me. There are no scars like the disaffections of one's household. After that my mother grieved no more over my radicalism, but because I never again would talk to her about my real and intimate concerns.

Fortunately, about that time my destiny took me into the adventure which is the chief source of that confident exuberance of spirit which no contact with this momentarily disillusioned world had ever been able to dim.

"I WAS IN THE STONE AGE"

In 1888, just out of college, I went to live in the California desert and began to know Indians. I became interested in them at first because there was literally nothing else human in my neighborhood to be interested in; and then because they were downtrodden. This is the normal progression of youth. While my contemporaries in more settled districts were beginning to sympathize with "labor," and walk with strikers, I fought the missionaries and the Indian Bureau alike for a square deal for the original Americans. In the midst of my finding out what constituted a square deal for the aborigine, suddenly a door opened on my path, and I knew where I was exactly. I was in the Stone Age, seeing the beginning of all the social muddle which has vexed my generation so sorely. Curious how I have never been able to get the radicals of my own day to realize this! I know that if a remnant of Europe's Stone Age were discovered, say in the Pyrenees, they would all go there, ex-economists and social philosophers alike, with note-books and acute curiosity. But I was there, in California, U.S.A., and nobody even wanted to hear about it.

For eighteen years I followed that trail with avidity. The business of tracing it clear to our own day governed my reading. I saw the beginning of institutionalized marriage out of natural monogamous mating as the species mark; the rise of capital, not out of greed and oppression as my urban contemporaries would have it, but out of the inescapable tendency of goods to accumulate around dominant personalities. I watched man's primitive struggle with this tendency, which actually, since it happened to him before wage labor was invented, he found clogging. I watched the development of the city-state, and the inevitable evolution of republicanism into communism, and saw communism die of its own inhibitions.

So far as I am able to discover, the only miscalculation in all my study was in supposing that contemporary radicalism was really interested in these things. By 1903–04, intermittent visits to San Francisco had brought me in touch with radicals, whose word for existing conditions I was inclined to accept. In 1906 I went to Europe, where I met radicals of various nationalities, had long talks with H. G. Wells, and heard Shaw and the Webbs at the Fabian Society. It was not until I reached New York, however, in 1909, that I discovered that the reason why none of the American radicals wished to hear about my excursions into the Stone Age, was that they thought they already knew everything.

That, in brief, seems to me to have been the trouble with prewar radicalism. It never was a radicalism that went to the roots, but back to a doctrinaire teaching; Karl Marx's for choice. It was paralyzingly sure not only of beginnings, but of ends. I recall with what shock I used to hear the New York radicals betting on the date of the unexpected social revolution, anywhere from two years to the day after tomorrow. Not even the profound sincerity of such expectation saved it from seeming, to a visitor from the Stone Age, absurd.

TOPSY-TURVY RADICALISM

One of the curiosities of prevailing radical faith was the want of logic in such naive ideas as have been honestly confessed by Fremont Older: that the economic regeneration of the world was to be accomplished by making the poor rich and the rich poor, as Russia has so tragically tried to demonstrate. The same illogicality prevailed in all ideas about sex; they were simply and splendidly reversed. Whereas formerly in marriage the privilege had devolved upon the faithful one, it was bestowed on the unfaithful. To be steadfast proved one limited; to resent a breach of faith, hysterical; mere instability of the affections alone was enough to demonstrate an advanced status. I have heard pre-war radicals so steeped in these absurdities that not even a sense of humor saved them. But all that has been honestly accounted for by Floyd Dell, and received absolution. What has not yet been delimited from the radicalism that evaporated, is the provincialism that still more or less touches all liberal thought that originates or makes its home continuously in New York. Many radicals of that time were so newly come to America that they suffered real incapacity to digest what they found on Manhattan Island alone, and resented my insistence in a deeper rootage further west. The idea that nothing really vital to social evolution can originate in any other place than that in which the intelligentsia happen to be congregated, is a dusty sediment from that vanished state of sociological enthusiasm, lying still over all our thought.

I was several years finding this out. . . .

A list of the several influential regional publications to come out of the American West, including the Overland Monthly *and Charles Lummis's* Out West, *must also include Willard H. (Spud) Johnson's literary itinerant,* Laughing Horse. *Published intermittently from 1921 to 1939, first in Berkeley, then in Guadalajara, and finally in Santa Fe and Taos,* Laughing Horse *has one of the most colorful and little-known publishing histories of any twentieth-century cultural journal.*

One of the magazine's many interesting moments came in 1930 in response to the controversy surrounding James Joyce's Ulysses *(1922), banned by the U.S. government as obscene. In 1929, Senator Bronson Cutting of New Mexico sponsored an amendment to the Tariff Act of 1890 that would finally allow Joyce's novel into the country, and in support, Johnson devoted the entire February 1930 issue of* Laughing Horse *to "A Symposium of Criticism, Comment and Opinion on the Subject of Censorship." Johnson assembled contributions from twenty-nine well-known figures in publishing and the arts, among them, Carl Sandburg, Mabel Dodge Luhan, Will Irwin, John Dewey, Harriet Monroe, Sherwood Anderson, Witter Bynner, Alfred A. Knopf, and Upton Sinclair, and he provided a brief parenthetical designation for each contributor, including "Mary Austin (Feminist)." All twenty-nine contributors sided with Cutting's proposal, and* Laughing Horse *was distributed in the U.S. Senate before the successful passage of the amendment. Austin's appeal in her short essay is to public-spiritedness and cooperation as much as it is to the preservation of freedom of speech.*

Censorship

In the midst of zeal either to defend or destroy freedom of speech as a constitutional right, both sides manage to overlook the grave consideration of such freedom as a social precaution. Yet if there is any such thing as a right to say what one thinks, it must depend upon the certainty that at all times and on most occasions, every human being is liable to the common mishap of thinking wrongly.

Probably there has never been anyone who could not be convicted of having at one time or another entertained ideas which have been pronounced or proven "bad," or at least grievously mistaken. Indeed, the primary requisite for a scientific career — science in general being the business of right thinking — is the ability and willingness to abandon publicly any idea, however long and sincerely entertained, the moment it is shown to be incorrect or otherwise inadmissable.

It is this liability to wrong thinking which binds us to the common obligation to refrain from exercising social compulsion on other people's thinking.

Without doubt, every one of the people who undertake to forbid the expression of ideas on sex or politics differing from their own, could be shown as entertaining ideas on sex or politics or public health or education or economics, which have already been pronounced "bad" by experts in those fields.

This is so generally understood that enlightened people the world over have agreed on Freedom of Speech as a sporting precaution.

Not to be willing to abide by this precaution of permitting free speech in the hope that some of us will eventually be found to be right, evinces an unsocial attitude which negates the whole principle of republicanism. I often ask myself whether organizations devoted to the suppression of opinion are not in their nature unconstitutional to the degree that would warrant their abo-

Originally published in the *Laughing Horse* 17 (1930). Reprinted by permission of the School of American Research.

lition. Or at least, could we not demand of them a pledge that every member hold himself willing, on being convicted of incorrect thinking on any other subject, to suffer the same fines and penalties prescribed for the thinkers they hope to suppress?

We might, then initiate a system of "pairing" in suppressions, similar to that employed in votes. I, for instance, would be glad to pair off my opposition to French corsets, now being introduced, with anyone entertaining a like antipathy to French novels or risque comedies, or the Old Testament. Or the societies opposed to the importation of foreign political ideals, could cancel out with the rage for the extirpation of alcoholic drink.

I am in favor of sharpening our weapons to pierce the moral obtuseness which hedges such organizations as the Watch and Ward Society and the Sumner forces, with a practical demonstration of what really happens when it is once admitted that no particular kind of wrong thinking is more sacred or exempt than any other.

The appearance of a leader of informed, intelligent public spiritedness, is a hopeful augury of being able to achieve our constitutionally guaranteed freedom by reasonable means.

Let us follow Senator Cutting as far as the present adventure leads. But it should never be overlooked that the American demand for "practicality" may yet demand of us an objective demonstration.

During the summer of 1933, Austin reiterated the ideas expressed in "Regionalism in American Fiction" at a conference on the topic of regional literature held at the University of Montana in Missoula. In response to a question, she reportedly claimed that even Milton's Paradise Lost *was regional in time. Although Austin wrote consistently of and about the American West, it is fair to say that this essay represents the core of Austin's formal theoretical thinking about the experience of the American West.*

Praising "fiction which has come up through the land, shaped by the author's own adjustments to it," Austin suggests that a strong regional sense in literature can act as a corrective to the "blurred" effects of what she saw, even in the 1930s, as an increasingly homogenized mass culture, or "the proverbial bird's-eye view of the American scene, what you might call an automobile eye view," as she refers to it here. Austin's thinking about regional issues participates in the larger movement of "regional reconstruction" promoted by many American intellectuals during the 1920s and 1930s. Expanding from the more limited "local color" school of the late nineteenth century and debating the theories of historian Frederick Jackson Turner, such writers and critics as Lewis Mumford and Vernon L. Parrington developed models of cultural decentralization that would find currency among both regional writers and social reformers during the Depression years. Austin was well aware of this general regional current surfacing in American letters at the time, perhaps most directly through the work of her friend Carey McWilliams, whose 1930 The New Regionalism in American Literature *was a reasoned defense of regional writing, stemming from his appreciation for the value in a romantic vision of primitive, agrarian, and otherwise former ways of life.*

Austin's "Regionalism" essay stands up interestingly against the so-called "frontier thesis" of Frederick Jackson Turner. In his well-known and much debated 1893 essay "The Significance of the Frontier in American History," Turner sees the then recent "closing" of the western frontier (official closing, that is, by decree of the United States Census Bureau in 1890) as a step away from the creative, formative role that the American West had once exerted in fashioning American thought and character. Austin, on the other hand, focuses on the ongoing influence of the region, detailing in her work a sense of a unique regional experience that in her view would have to form the basis for human occupation of the West in the twentieth century.

Regionalism in American Fiction

"Regionalism in literature," says Dorothy Canfield in a recent review of what she considers an excellent example of it, "is the answer to the problem of getting any literature at all out of so vast and sprawling a country as ours." She might as truthfully have said it of any art and any country which is large enough to cover more than one type of natural environment. Art, considered as the expression of any people as a whole, is the response they make in various mediums to the impact that the totality of their experience makes upon them, and there is no sort of experience that works so constantly and subtly upon man as his regional environment. It orders and determines all the direct, practical ways of his getting up and lying down, of staying in and going out, of housing and clothing and food-getting; it arranges by its progressions of seed times and harvest, its rain and wind and burning suns, the rhythms of his work and amusements. It is the thing always before his eye, always at his ear, always underfoot. Slowly or sharply it forces upon him behavior patterns such as earliest become the habit of his blood, the unconscious factor of adjustment in all his mechanisms. Of all the responses of his psyche, none pass so soon and surely as these into that field of consciousness from which all invention and creative effort of every sort proceed. Musical experts say that they can trace a racial influence in composition many generations back, and what is a race but a pattern of response common to a group of people who have lived together under a given environment long enough to take a recognizable pattern?

Everybody has known this a long time. We have known it about classic Greek and ancient Egypt. We know that the distinctions between Scotch and Irish and British literature have not been erased, have scarcely been touched by their long association of all three under one political identity; we know in fact that at last the pattern of Irish regionalism has prevailed over polity, and

Originally published in the *English Journal* 21 (1932) by the National Council of Teachers of English. Reprinted by permission of the School of American Research.

it is still a problem of the Irish Free State to withstand the separative influences of regionalism on their own green island. We recognize Moorish and Iberian elements in Spanish art, at the same time that we fully realize something distinctive that comes to this mixed people out of the various regional backgrounds within the Spanish peninsula. Knowing all this, it is rather surprising to find critics in the United States speaking of regionalism as something new and unprecedented in a territory so immensely varied as ours. The really astonishing thing would have been to find the American people as a whole resisting the influence of natural environment in favor of the lesser influences of a shared language and a common political arrangement.

Actually this notion, that the American people should differ from all the rest of the world in refusing to be influenced by the particular region called home, is a late by-product of the Civil War and goes with another ill-defined notion that there is a kind of disloyalty in such a differentiation and an implied criticism in one section of all the others from which it is distinguished. It would be easy to trace out the growth of such an idea, helped as it is and augmented in its turn by the general American inability to realize the source of all art as deeper than political posture, arising, as people truly and rudely say, in our "guts," the seat of life and breath and heartbeats, of loving and hating and rearing. It is not in the nature of mankind to be all of one pattern in these things any more than it is in the nature of the earth to be all plain, all seashore, or all mountains. Regionalism, since it is of the very nature and constitution of the planet, becomes at last part of the nature and constitution of the men who live on it.

Since already a sense of the truth of these things, as applicable to our own country, has worked through to the common consciousness, our real concern is not to argue the case, but to fortify ourselves against the possibility of our missing the way again by failing to discriminate between a genuine regionalism and mistaken presentiments of it. We need to be prompt about it, before somebody discovers that our resistance so far has been largely owed to intellectual laziness which flinches from the task of competently knowing, not one vast, pale figure of America, but several Americas, in many subtle and significant characterizations.

As a matter of fact, our long disappointed expectation of the "great American novel," for which every critic was once obliged to keep an eye out, probably originated in the genuine inability of the various regions to see greatness in novels that dealt with fine and subtle distinctions in respect to some other region. But we have only to transfer the wishful thinking for a single book, or a single author, who would be able to overcome our inextinguishable ignorance of each other, to Europe to become aware of its absurdity. To Europeans our American regional differentiations, all comprised under one language and one government, are very puzzling. That is one reason why they have seized so promptly on *Main Street* and especially on *Babbitt* as just the broad, thin, generalized surface reflection of the American community and American character which the casual observer receives. Babbitt is an American type, the generalized, "footless" type which has arisen out of a rather wide-spread resistance to regional interests and influences, out of a determined fixation on the most widely shared, instead of the deepest rooted, types of American activity. That Babbitt is exactly that sort of person and that he is unhappy in being it, is probably exactly what Mr. Lewis meant to show. But that millions of Americans rise up to reject him as representing "our part of the country" only goes to show that, deep down and probably unconsciously, all the time that one set of influences has been shaping the shallow Babbitt citizen, another set has been at work to produce half a dozen other regionally discriminated types for whom there is, naturally, no common literary instance.

Perhaps the country does not fully realize that in rejecting Babbitt as our family name, it has declared for the regional types such as the best American fictionists have already furnished us. Probably the American reading public never has understood that its insistence on fiction shallow enough to be common to all regions, so that no special knowledge of other environments than one's own is necessary to appreciation of it, has pulled down the whole level of American fiction. It is more than likely that even the critics, who can be discovered surrendering to the idea of strongly marked regional fiction, have no notion of the work they are cutting out for themselves under the necessity of knowing good regional books when they see them. But there it is, the recognition and the demand. People of the South aren't satisfied to go on forever reading novels about New York and Gopher Prairie, people of the Pacific Coast want occasionally to read "something more like us." They are willing to be tolerant and even interested in other regions on consideration that they get an occasional fair showing for themselves.

Fortunately, if we go back far enough, we have plenty of regional fiction to furnish a prototype and a criterion of criticism. It is, in fact, the only sort of fiction that will bear reading from generation to generation. Any confirmed novel reader of more than a generation's experience, or any teacher of English, should be able to name a score of them offhand. I begin my own list with *Queechy* as the best novel of rural life in New England ever written. I should begin with one of Herman Melville's, except that I am trying to omit for the moment regionalism which has also a narrow time limit; the environment of the whaler's sea that Melville knew has already been eaten up in time. I would name Hawthorne's *The House of the Seven Gables* rather than *The Scarlet Letter*, the latter being less of the land and more of the temper of Puritanism, more England than New England. To these I would add something of that gifted author of *The Country of the Pointed Firs*, Sarah Orne Jewett. Of Henry James, *Washington Square* most definitely fulfills the regional test of not being possible to have happened elsewhere. Out of New York I would choose *The House of Mirth*; but we have Hergesheimer's *Three Black Pennys* and *Balisand* and James Branch Cabell's least known, and to my think, best, *The Rivet in Grandfather's Neck*. When Mr. Cabell tells us the true story of why he never wrote another like it, but invented the region of Poictesme in old France against which to display his literary gifts, we shall know many revealing things about the influences shaping literature in the United States.

In the Mississippi Valley, one thinks at once of *Tom Sawyer* and Huckleberry Finn. Along the Middle Border there are Hamlin Garland's earlier tales, such as *Main Travelled roads*; and on the edge of the plains are Ed Howe's neglected masterpiece, *The Story of a Country Town*, and Willa Cather's *My Antonia*. Of the

Southwest, unless you will accept the present writer's *Starry Adventure*, there is as yet very little genuinely representative — not that there are not stories of that country which are well worth the reading, and at least one immortal short story, Stephen Crane's *The Bride Comes to Yellow Sky*. Our Southwest, though actually the longest-lived-in section of the country, has not yet achieved its authentic literary expression in English. On the California coast there are a number of entirely characteristic short stories. Chester Bailey Fernald's *The Cat and the Cherub* comes instantly to mind, and at least two of Frank Norris' novels.

This is to name only those titles which occur irresistibly in this connection — fiction which has come up through the land, shaped by the author's own adjustments to it — and leave out many excellent and illuminating works which are colored, not only by the land, but by the essence of a period, a phase of its social development, a racial bias, a time element too short to develop essential characteristics. Such as these are the stories of George W. Cable, and Grace Medard King of Old Louisiana, Bret Harte's tales of "Forty-Nine," and such delicate but inerasable sketches as F. Hopkinson Smith's *Colonel Carter of Cartersville*. I should think, indeed, that an importantly readable anthology of tales dealing with these local rather than regional shorter phases of American life could be easily gathered; but I am concerned chiefly to establish a criterion of what is first class regional fiction than to name every item that could possibly be included in that category. Lovers of W. D. Howells will wonder why his name does not appear here. If it belongs here, it is largely on account of *Silas Lapham*. Many sections of America could have produced Silas, but the things that happened to him in Howells' story could have happened only in Boston, and in that sense it is a true regional expression, and very likely will be estimated as Howells' best piece, chiefly because it has the deep-rooted motivation which is the essential quality of regionalism. But it has always seemed to me that Howells was the first, and the most eminent, of the American novelists responsible for the thinning out of American fiction by a deliberate choice of the most usual, the most widely distributed of American story incidents, rather than the most intensively experienced. Between Howells and Sinclair Lewis we have the whole history of that excursion of the American novelist away from the soil, undertaken on the part of Howells in a devout pilgrim spirit, bent on the exploration of the social expression of democracy, and on the part of Lewis with a fine scorn and a hurt indignation for the poor simp who, having filled his belly with husks, does not yet know enough to say, "I will arise and go to my father."

In all this instancing of archetypes, we must by no means leave out the books for children which belong in this list, and more than any other sort of literature overlap in the lists. We begin chronologically with Cooper's tales, of which half a dozen are absolute types, and then think at once of *Tom Sawyer* and *Huckleberry Finn*. It is only because the Alcott books are less picaresque that we fail to realize them as not the less regional, possible only to a long settled culture, so much longer settled than most American cultures at the time they were written, that much of their charm for the country at large lay in the note of nostalgia for the richer and more spiritual life which they aroused. This writer, who read them as they came fresh from the pen of the Boston spinster, knows well how intimately they presented the social and moral aspirations of the still crude Middle West of that time. It is their profound fidelity to what was the general American feeling for the best in family life that makes the Alcott stories still moving and popular. It is the greatest mistake in the world not to recognize that children are affected by these things, being at heart the most confirmed regionalists. What they like as background for a story is an explicit, well mapped strip of country, as intensively lived into as any healthy child lives into his own neighborhood.

Two other writers of my youth, who might well be kept on the children's list, were Eggleston and Trowbridge, along with half a dozen of the stories of Mayme Reid. If I name nothing modern it is because my acquaintance with modern literature for children is too scanty for me to feel sure of naming the best. When I was young the best of everything appeared in *St. Nicholas*; and the best was always explicitly localized, dealt with particular birds and beasts, trees and growing things, incidents that had their source in four great causatives: climate, housing, transportation, and employment.

There is, for children, another region, often completely closed to their elders, for which the same rules hold. I mean the world of fairy adventure. Grown up people often make the oddest, most lamentable mistakes in attempting to deal with this world; the most unforgivable is to treat it as though there were no rules, no such thing as fairy logic. The fact is that this fairy world is precisely the grown-up world as it presented itself to the childhood of the race. To be wholly satisfying, stories of this world must be made to hang together as it hung together for our ancestors of the Stone Age. Fortunately the very greatest geniuses among fairy-world realists, like Lewis Carroll, Hans Christian Anderson, and Rudyard Kipling, are perfectly aware of the regional rules and never violate them in the least particular. In the *Jungle Book*, tigers are always true to their tigerishness and wolves to the imaginary lore of the pack. Mr. Kipling's jungle may not be the verifiable jungle of India, nor even of little Hindu girls and boys, but it is the complete jungle of the childhood of the race. Mowgli is as full of forest guile as any other young animal, and as completely innocent of heart, so that the young reader shares with him every thrill of the daily hunt and kill, without ever once realizing that what Mowgli eats is hot raw meat which he tears apart with his teeth and hands. A writer less able to understand innocence of heart than Mr. Kipling would have conscientiously tried to make a complete vegetarian of him.

In the same way the countries down the rabbit hole and behind the looking glass never depart for an instant from fidelity to the topsy-turviness of the land of dreams. No item except such as a perfectly normal little girl like Alice might take with her into dreamland is ever allowed to intrude incongruously into the story. These two regions of our Ancestral European past and topsy-turvy-dream are by this time so well mapped that it is sheer stupidity for a writer to go astray in them. But there is another story-region to which every American child has right of access, all the laws of which have been so violated by well-meaning and ill-informed writers, that it ought to be a penal offense to keep on doing so — I mean the world of American Indian lore. This world begins in the door-yard of every American child; it can be fully entered at the edge of every American town, it can be looked out upon from every train window and crossed by every automobile. But so ignorant of this region are most grown up Americans, that there are but three guides to whom I could unhesitatingly recommend the exploring child to trust: Joel Chandler Harris, James Willard Schultz, and Arthur Parker. There are, of course, individual works, such as Frank Hamilton Cushing's *Zuñi Folk Tales*, which are absolute in their transcription of Indian regionalism.

But the trouble with ninety-nine out of every hundred Indian books offered to American children is that their authors fail to know that everything an Indian does or thinks is patterned by the particular parcel of land which is his tribal home. Thus at its very source the processes of regional culture, from which the only sound patriotism springs, are corrupted by the same inchoate jumble of environmental elements which so irritates us when pointed out by distinguished foreigners.

Until within the last twenty years the literary expectation of the United States could be quite simply allocated to New England; New York City; a "misty midregion" known as the Middlewest, as weird as Weir and not any more explicitly mapped; to which append the fringing Old South and the Far West. At the present, the last two have completely receded into the dimension of time past, The Old South has given rise to the New South; the Far West has split into the Southwest, the Northwest, the California Coast, and the Movie West. Cleavages begin to appear in the Middlewest, outlining *The Great Meadow*, the title of the best book about the section just south of Ohio. Farther north lies the Middle Border and Chicago. Within New York City we are aware of the East Side and Harlem which is the capital of the new Negro world, each producing its own interpreters. Even in the Indian region there is faint indication of splitting off from the children's Indian country of a meagerly explored adult interest.

To the average citizen, notice of these recent annexations to the literary world comes in the form of a new book which everybody is talking about, dealing with life as it is lived there, as it unmistakably couldn't be lived anywhere else. And immediately the average citizen who, however much he wishes to read what everybody else is reading, secretly hankers to be able to discriminate for himself, begins to cast about for a criterion of what acceptable regionalism in literature should be. For to be able to speak of the credibility of reports of the various countries contained within our country requires a nimble wit and a considerable capacity for traveling in one's mind. How, the reader inquires inwardly, without having lived it myself, shall I feel certain that this book does give in human terms the meaning of that country in which the action of the story takes place? One might answer shortly, by the same means that it has become a proverb in the country where I live that "a wool grower knows a wool buyer." Whoever has lived deeply and experientially into his own environment, is by so much the better prepared to recognize the same experience in another. But there are criteria not to be ignored for recognizing regionalism in literature.

The first of the indispensable conditions is that the region must enter constructively into the story, as another character, as the instigator of plot. A natural scene can never be safely assumed to be the region of the story when it is used merely as a backdrop — not that the scenic backdrop cannot be used effectively by way of contrast, or to add a richer harmonization to a story shaped by alien scenes. Henry James is master of this trick, as when in *The Golden Bowl* he uses aristocratic England as a setting for a group of rich Americans and one Italian Prince; or, as in *The Ambassadors*, he unfolds a New England complication against smart Paris. Edith Wharton does it less handsomely in *The Children*, and Sinclair Lewis less importantly in *Dodsworth*. Willa Cather does it most appealingly in *Death Comes for the Archbishop*. I am often asked if this last is not what I mean by a "regional" book of the Southwest. Not in the least. The hero is a missionary arriving here at an age when the major patterns of his life are already set; a Frenchman by birth, a Catholic by conviction and practice, a priest by vocation, there is little that New Mexico can do for him besides providing him an interesting backdrop against which to play out his missionary part. Miss Cather selects her backgrounds with care, draws them with consummate artistry, in this case perverting the scenes from historical accuracy, and omitting — probably, herself, in complete ignorance of it — the tragic implications of its most significant item and so makes it convincing for her audience. I am not saying that his is not a legitimate literary device. That Archbishop Lamy, who was the historic prototype of Miss Cather's leading character, also missed the calamity to Spanish New Mexican culture, of the coming of the French priests, is the one profoundly human touch that so competent a literary artist as Miss Cather should not have overlooked. It makes her story, with all its true seeming, profoundly untrue to the New Mexican event, which removes it from the category of regional literature.

One of the likeliest mistakes the inexperienced reader will make in allocating books to their proper regional source, is to select stories about the region rather than of it. Such a reader would for example class *Uncle Tom's Cabin* as a southern book, when, in fact, its approach, its moral and intellectual outlook is New England from the ground up, and so are its most telling characters. The South never saw itself in Harriet Beecher Stowe's light, never looked on slavery as she displayed it. Southerners would not deny the book's regional character, but they are still protesting after nearly three-quarters of a century that it is not of their region. In the same manner, old Californians, forty years ago, could be heard denying the regional authenticity of *Ramona*. They recognized neither themselves nor their Indians in Helen Hunt Jackson's presentation. The regionally interpretive book must not only be about the country, it must be of it, flower of its stalk and root, in the way that *Huckleberry Finn* is of the great river, taking its movement and rhythm, its structure and intention, or lack of it, from the scene. In the way that Edna Ferber's *Cimarron* isn't of the land but pleasingly and reasonably about it.

With these two indispensable conditions of the environment entering constructively into the story, and the story reflecting in some fashion the essential qualities of the land, it is not easy to put one's finger on representative regional fiction. *Slow Smoke* by Charles Malam is the novel Dorothy Canfield mentions. A book I have in mind as fulfilling all the conditions competently is

Frank Applegate's *Indian Stories from the Pueblos*. These are native tales which he tells in the manner in which the natives would tell them. Work of this kind comes on slowly. Time is the essence of the undertaking, time to live into the land and absorb it; still more time to cure the reading public of its preference for something less than the proverbial bird's-eye view of the American scene, what you might call an automobile eye view, something slithering and blurred, nothing so sharply discriminated that it arrests the speed-numbed mind to understand, characters like garish gas stations picked out with electric lights. The one chance of persuading the young reader to make these distinctions for himself would be to whet his appreciation on the best regional literature of our past so that he may not miss the emerging instance of his own times.

Austin wrote this short essay as an introduction to a collection of her Indian stories, what Austin might have called her "reexpressions" of Native American sensibilities, published in the Yale Review. Austin uses the intriguing expression "one smoke story" to describe a story meant to be told during the span of smoking one ceremonial cigarette. The title suggests the occasion and dynamic personal interaction of storytelling. It records Austin's appreciation of the vitality of Native American orality and her sometimes controversial appropriation and interpretation of indigenous culture.

There may be another source as well. Austin spent much of her life in Los Angeles, Carmel, New York, London, and Santa Fe, among the artists, writers, publishers, political activists, and impresarios whom we remember as the creative, flamboyant, combative intelligentsia of the early twentieth century. Imagine, for example, the electric exchange of ideas during Mabel Dodge Luhan's Wednesday night "evenings" in Greenwich Village. Max Eastman did his best to preserve their spirit of discussion in his 1927 novel Venture. Carl Van Vechten draws upon them in his 1922 Peter Whiffle. Mabel Dodge Luhan herself gives good account in her 1936 Movers and Shakers. Austin's own sense of oral culture, described in the idiom of the indigenous culture she so passionately admired and fostered, inevitably draws upon her own experience as well, for she both contributed to and listened to what may have been some of the most stimulating conversation of the century.

The same issue of the Yale Review contains Henry Tracy's reviews of Earth Horizon and Hamlin Garland's My Friendly Contemporaries. Tracy admired Austin's autobiography, which unlike Garland's was "no passive picture, but an imaginative reconstruction charged with dramatic force." Tracy adds that Austin's "struggle" "might seem personal, or merely feminist, if it were not cosmic in its implications."[1]

Appearing the year before her death, Austin's introduction, particularly its understated closing, suggests much about the spirit in which she understood her own work and provides a fitting conclusion to a glimpse of that work as seen in a collection of her essays.

One Smoke Stories

The corn-husk cigarettes, which for ceremonial purposes are still used south of Green River and west of the Rio Grande, last only a little while. Since they are filled with the biting native *tabac*, this is perhaps not to be regretted. You select your husk from the heap and gather your pinch of the weed from the dark bowl as it passes the ancient ceremonial road from east to north by west to south, and holding the dry roll delicately between your lips endeavor to dispatch the salutary puffs to the six, or, if you happen to be among the Navajo, the four world quarters. Try as you may, you will probably never master the unobtrusive art, though I have seen white men whose standing in the country is that of "old timers" allowing the smoke to escape from their lips in the appointed directions, but in such a manner that they are able, if you accuse one of them of it, to deny it successfully.

Thus after a day of preparation for the unending seasonal rituals that keep the Indian snug in his environment, sib to it, in the old sense of communicable, answering back again, around the embers sit the meditative Elders. Now and again holding the crisp cylinder between thumb and finger tip, unlit, one begins, always gravely, and holds on, for the space of one smoke, tales each as deft, as finished in itself, as a ceremonial cigarette. Or if not a tale, then a clean round out of the speaker's experience, such as in our kind of society, might turn up a sonnet or an etching. And between them, the ingoing and outgoing sense of the universe pulses and spirals with the ascending smoke.

The essence of all such stories is that they should be located somewhere in the inner sense of the audience, unencumbered by what in our more discursive method is known as background.

Your true desert dweller travels light. He makes even of his experience a handy package, with the finished neatness that distinguishes his artifacts. How else could they be passed intact from tribe to tribe, from generation to generation? Just before the end,

Originally published in the *Yale Review* 22 (1933). Reprinted by permission of Blackwell Publishers.

like the rattle which warns that the story is about to strike, comes the fang of the experience, most often in the shape of a wise saying. Then the speaker resumes the soul consoling smoke, while another takes up the dropped stitch of narrative and weaves it into the pattern of the talk.

Folk experience admits many tellable items which, in a world of pretentious sophistication like ours, are inhibited. It admits the friendly dead, the talking animal whose wisdom is profounder than ours because his mysteriousness is nearer to the Great Mystery. It admits the Surpassing Beings whom we blunderingly designate as Gods — the Sacred Trues who are themselves the instigators of experience. Some of the tales most esteemed by the audiences that originally heard them are unintelligible to our so much more objective minds. They dip too deeply, pass beyond our ken into that region mastery over which man resigned as the purchase price of intelligence. Others, and these are often the wittiest, are inhibited by our proprieties. Not that I was ever told anything unsuitable for a woman to hear, but between their suitabilities and ours is all the distance we have travelled to know that the joke the Trues placed upon man when they tied procreation to responsibility is not a joke to women.

As for the manner of telling, I hope I shall be found adhering closely to the original method, but if occasionally I am discovered adding to the austere relation such further perception of the scene as is necessary to have the fang of the story strike home, I shall hope it is not too much. In the words of the sacred formula: I give you to smoke.

NOTE

1. *Yale Review* 22 (1933).

The most comprehensive list of Austin's magazine publications is found in Joseph Gaer, *Mary Austin: Bibliography and Biographical Data*, Monograph No. 2. (Berkeley: Library Research Digest, 1934). The following is provided to guide more general reading.

"Aboriginal Fiction." *Saturday Review of Literature* 6 (1929).

"The American Form of the Novel." *New Republic* 30 (1922).

"American Indian Dance Drama." *Yale Review* 19 (1930).

"American Indian Murals." *American Magazine of Art* 26 (1933).

"American Women and the Intellectual Life." *Bookman* 53 (1921).

"Amerindian Folklore." *Bookman* 56 (1922).

"An Appreciation of H. G. Wells, Novelist." *American Magazine* 72 (1911).

"Arizona: The Land of Joyous Adventure." *Nation* 116 (1923).

"Art Influence in the West." *Century Magazine* 89 (1915).

"Artist Life in the United States." *Nation* 120 (1925).

"Automatism in Writing." *Unpartizan Review* 14 (1920).

"Best Twenty Years." *Survey* 60 (1928).

"Beyond the Hudson." *Saturday Review of Literature* 7 (1930).

"Buck and Wing and Bill Hudson." *Nation* 122 (1926).

"Can Prayer be Answered?" *Forum* 91 (1934).

"Cantu in Baja California." *Nation* 111 (1920).

"Censorship." *Laughing Horse* 17 (1930).

"A Child Must Have Some Kind of Religion." *Pictorial Review* 29 (1928).

"The Colorado River." *Century Magazine* 108 (1924).

"The Colorado River Controversy." *Nation* 125 (1927).

"Community Make-Believe." *Good Housekeeping* Aug. 1914.

"Cults of the Pueblos." *Century Magazine* 109 (1924).

"The Days of Our Ancients." *Survey* 53 (1923).

"Do We Need a New Religion." *Century Magazine* 100 (1923).

"A Drama Played on Horseback." *Mentor* 16 (1928).

"English Book and American Reviewers." *Bookman* (London) 61 (1922).

"Experiences Facing Death." *Forum* 80 (1928).

"Folk Literature." *Saturday Review of Literature* 5 (1928).

"Folk Plays of the Southwest." *Theatre Arts Magazine* 17 (1933).

"The Folly of the Officials." *Forum* 71 (1924).

"Food Conservation and the Women." *Unpopular Review* 9 (1918).

"The Forward Turn." *Nation* 125 (1927).

"The Future of the Southwest." *New Republic* 42 (1925).

"George Sterling at Carmel." *American Mercury* 11 (1927).

"Gesture in Primitive Drama." *Theatre Arts Magazine* 11 (1927).

"Greatness in Women." *North American Review* 217 (1923).

"Historical Memorial." *Commonweal* 16 (1934).

"Hoover and Johnson: West is West." *Nation* 110 (1920).

"How I Found the Thing Worth Waiting For." *Survey* 61 (1929).

"Hunt of Arizona." *Nation* 127 (1928).

"Indian Arts for Indians." *Survey* 60 (1928).

"The Indivisible Utility." *Survey* 55 (1925).

"Jimville — A Bret Harte Town." *Atlantic Monthly* 91 (1903).

"A Land of Little Rain." *Atlantic Monthly* 91 (1903).

"The Little Town of the Grape Vines." *Atlantic Monthly* 91 (1903).

"The Lone Woman Goes to War." *Los Angeles Times* 28 April 1918.

"Making the Most of Your Genius, I: What is Genius?" *Bookman* 58 (1923).

"Making the Most of Your Genius, II: Training Your Talent." *Bookman* 58 (1924).

"Making the Most of Your Genius, III: The Education of the Writer." *Bookman* 58 (1924).

"The Man Jesus." *North American Review* 201 (1915).

"Mary Austin on Marrying Successfully." *Los Angeles Times World Magazine*, 15 Dec. 1912.

"The Meter of Aztec Verse." *Southwest Review* 14 (1928).

"Mexicans and New Mexico." *Survey* 66 (1931).

"Mexico for the Mexicans." *World Outlook* 2 (1916).

"My Fabian Summer." *Bookman* 54 (1921).

"Mysticism and Jesus." *Century Magazine* 109 (1924).

"Native Drama in New Mexico." *Theatre Arts Magazine* 13 (1929).

"The Need for a New Social Concept." *New Republic* 26 (1922).

"New Mexican Spanish." *Saturday Review of Literature* 7 (1931).

"New York: Dictator of American Criticism." *Nation* 111 (1920).

"On the American Scene." *Saturday Review of Literature* 5 (1928).

"On Discovering Greatness." *Saturday Review of Literature* 6 (1929).

"One Hundred Miles on Horseback." *Blackburnian* 1889.

"One Smoke Stories." *Yale Review* 22 (1933).

"A Poet in Outland." *Overland Monthly* 85 (1927).

"Poetry in the Education of Children." *Bookman* 68 (1928).

"Poetry that Children Choose." *Saturday Review of Literature* 5 (1928).

"Primitive Man." *Forum* 78 (1927).

"Primitive Stage Setting." *Theatre Arts Magazine* 12 (1928).

"Regional Culture in the Southwest." *Southwest Review* 14 (1929).

"Regionalism in American Fiction." *English Journal* 21 (1932).

"Religion in the United States." *Century Magazine* 104 (1922).

"Rural Education in New Mexico." *University of New Mexico Bulletin* 2 (1931).

"Science for the Unscientific." *Bookman* 55 (1922).

"The Sense of Humor in Women." *New Republic* 41 (1924).

"Sermon in One Man." *Harper's Weekly* 58 (1914).

"Sex Emancipation Through War." *Forum* 59 (1918).

"Sex in American Literature." *Bookman* 57 (1923).

"Sir James Barrie, The Writer Who Never Grew Up." *Ladies Home Journal*
    Dec. 1921.

"The Situation in Sonora." *Nation* 110 (1920).

"Songs of the American Indian." *Harper's* 143 (1921).

"Sources of Poetic Influence in the Southwest." *Poetry* 43 (1933).

"Supernaturals in Fiction." *Unpartizan Review* 13 (1920).

"The Town That Doesn't Want a Chautauqua." *New Republic* 47 (1926).

"Training Children for Happy Marriages." *Harper's Weekly* 58 (1914).

"Wanted: A New Method in Mexico." *Nation* 110 (1920).

"Where We Get Tammany Hall and Carnegie Libraries." *World Outlook* 4 (1918).

"Why Americanize the Indian?" *Forum* 82 (1929).

"Why I Live in Santa Fe." *Golden Book* 16 (1932).

"Woman Alone." *Nation* 124 (1927).

"Woman and Her War Loot." *Sunset: The Pacific Monthly* 42 (1919).

"Woman Looks at Her World." *Pictorial Review* 26 (1924).

"Woman's Preferred Candidate." *Collier's Magazine* 29 May 1920.

"Women as Audience." *Bookman* 55 (1922).

"Women's Clubs To-day and To-morrow." *Ladies Home Journal* June 1922.

REUBEN J. ELLIS received his Ph.D. from the University of Colorado at Boulder and is an assistant professor of English at Hope College, where he teaches American literature and ethnic literature. His work focuses on the western United States, and his essays on western American writers, including Mary Austin, appear in several journals and collections.